W9-ALJ-487

trash-to-treasure
papermaking

trash-to-treasure
papermaking

make your own recycled paper from
newspapers & magazines / can & bottle labels /
discarded gift wrap / old phone books /
junk mail / comic books / and more...

Arnold E. Grummer

Storey Publishing

SOMERSET CO. LIBRARY
BRIDGEWATER, N.J. 08807

The mission of Storey Publishing is to serve our customers by publishing practical information that encourages personal independence in harmony with the environment.

Edited by Deborah Balmuth and Nancy D. Wood
Art direction and book design by Dan O. Williams
Photography by © Greg Nesbit Photography, except for pages 10, 12, 13, 15, 97, 207 courtesy of the author; 75 (scrap paper), 176 by Mars Vilaubi
Indexed by Nancy D. Wood

© 2011 by Arnold Grummer

All rights reserved. No part of this book may be reproduced without written permission from the publisher, except by a reviewer who may quote brief passages or reproduce illustrations in a review with appropriate credits; nor may any part of this book be reproduced, stored in a retrieval system, or transmitted in any form or by any means — electronic, mechanical, photocopying, recording, or other — without written permission from the publisher.

The information in this book is true and complete to the best of our knowledge. All recommendations are made without guarantee on the part of the author or Storey Publishing. The author and publisher disclaim any liability in connection with the use of this information.

Storey books are available for special premium and promotional uses and for customized editions. For further information, please call 1-800-793-9396.

Storey Publishing
210 MASS MoCA Way
North Adams, MA 01247
www.storey.com

Printed in China by R.R. Donnelley
10 9 8 7 6 5 4 3 2 1

Library of Congress Cataloging-in-Publication Data

Grummer, Arnold E., 1923–
  Trash-to-Treasure Papermaking / By Arnold E. Grummer.
    pages cm
  Includes bibliographical references and index.
   ISBN 978-1-60342-547-6 (pbk. : alk. paper)
  1. Paper, Handmade. 2. Papermaking. I. Title.
TS1124.5.G78 2011
676'.22—dc22
                                    2010043056

contents

Chapter 4
Recycling Techniques

60

Chapter 5
Pulp Magic

72

Chapter 6
More Fun Things to Try

92

Chapter 7 — 120
Paper Casting

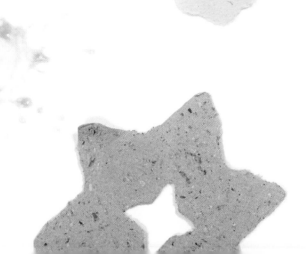

Chapter 8 — 146
Making Things with Paper

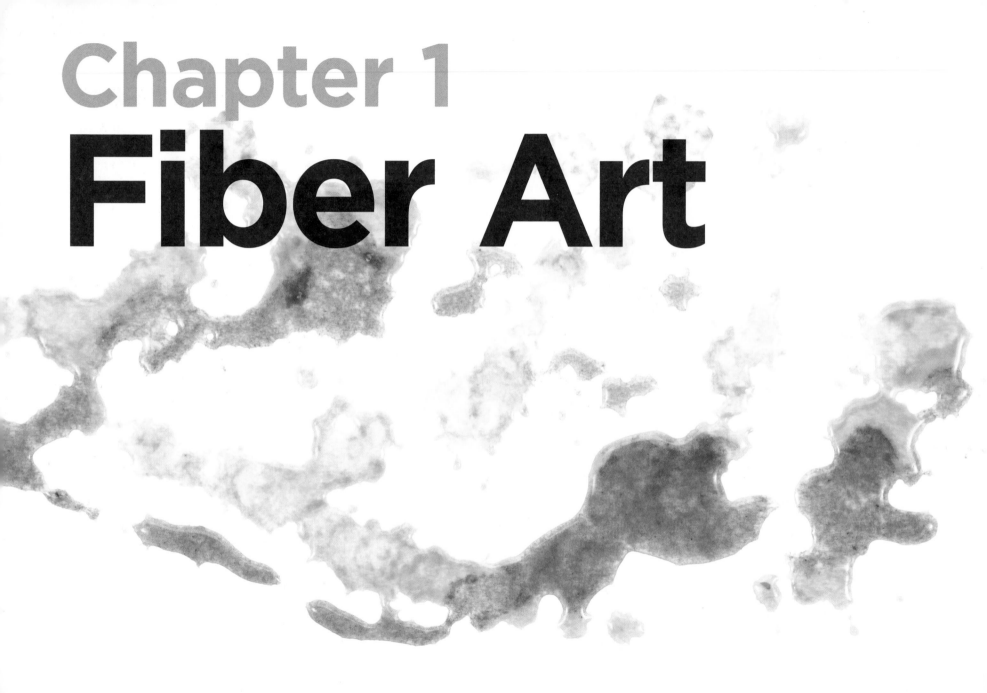

Chapter 1
Fiber Art

Where does paper come from? As you read these words, it appears as though the paper they're printed on is a fairly solid, unchanging object. But if you look more closely at the paper, through a magnifying glass or microscope, you may be able to see that this thin sheet of paper is actually made up of multiple layers of tiny fibers that have bonded together naturally. In the process of making paper, batches of single fibers are laid down into a thin, even mat.

So, you are holding a batch of little fibers. Across the fibers' backs, we have put ink in certain patterns. Behold, you and I can communicate!

The Nature of Plant Fibers

Paper fibers are cellulose. They are produced by everything that grows, from mighty trees to fungus and algae. Some people believe they are the most abundant thing on the face of the earth. The fibers used in papermaking are tiny: If you have very fine hair and were to cut off a ⅛″ piece, you would have something like a paper-making fiber.

Even though it's tiny, a cellulose fiber is hollow, like a drinking straw. If the cut surface of a tree stump were magnified a hundred times, you would be able to see all the little open-ended fibers lying side-by-side. Most fibers flatten out when made into paper, but some retain the hollow center.

Starting from Scratch

The first thing a commercial papermaker needs is processed fibers. In a process called *pulping*, all the cellulose fibers are forced loose from each other. Separating fibers is not easy. They hang together very strongly and must be separated using a grindstone, chemicals, or both.

Once the fibers have been separated, they are floated in water. This way, the papermaker can control where the fibers go and what they do. The fibers will go where the water goes. The papermaker keeps them separated in water and then pours the water onto a sieve with a rim around it. The rim channels water onto the sieve so

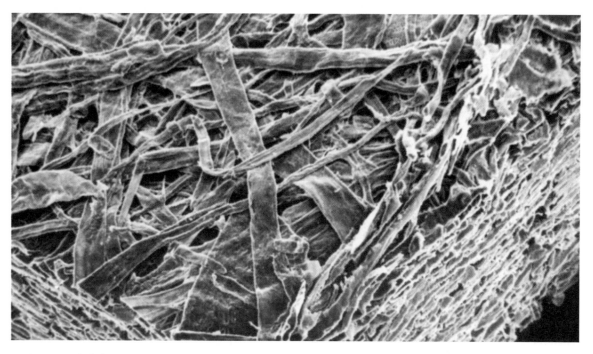

In this magnified photo, you can see the many layers of fibers that make up one thin sheet of paper.

it doesn't run off the sides. As water runs through the sieve, the single fibers are caught on the surface. That is how a papermaker lays down millions of little fibers in a thin, even mat.

The cellulose fibers that make up a sheet of paper are held together by a natural bond that happens when fibers touch each other in water. Very weak when formed, the bond grows stronger as water is *taken away*. The more water that is taken away, the stronger the bond becomes. When totally dry, the fibers are joined in a new sheet of paper.

Using Recycled Fibers

To make new paper from old, like we do in this book, a papermaker simply reverses the papermaking process. Dry paper is put into water, and the natural bond is weakened. The more water that is absorbed, the weaker the bond gets. It gets so weak that when the water is agitated (as in a blender), the fibers will let go of each other, once again becoming single fibers in water. This is called pulp. When pulp is poured onto a sieve and made into paper, it finishes a complete cycle: from new fibers to paper, from paper back to individual fibers, then those fibers are made into new paper. That is recycling.

Pulping Fibers

In the early days of papermaking, fibers were often ripped apart by stamping or grinding plants while wet. Sometimes the plants were soaked first in lime pits or water in which ashes had been soaked. Early grinding was done with a mortar and pestle. Later, machinery was developed. Today, your newspaper is made with fibers ripped apart by forcing a length of log against a grindstone. The fibers are then called *groundwood pulp*. Also, fibers can be obtained from trees and other plants by the use of chemicals or a combination of chemicals and grinding.

A Bit of History

Paper was first recorded as an invention in 105 AD, in China. This was linked to a man named Ts'ai Lun, an official in the Emperor's court. Many believed that Ts'ai Lun was the inventor of paper, but paper was probably being made before him.

Dard Hunter, master paper historian (*see* He Saved Paper's History *on the next page*), believed the first paper was made by floating a hand mold on the surface of calm water. The mold was likely made from

a piece of fabric stretched on a bamboo frame. Pulp was poured onto the fabric, and the mold was lifted from the water. The water drained, leaving a layer of fibers on the fabric. When the fiber layer dried, it was paper. Because pulp was poured into the hand mold, the method became known as the *pour* method.

Later on, a different method was developed: A large batch of pulp was put into a vat, and sheets were formed by dipping a hand mold into the vat. This became known as the *dip* method. The dip method began to replace the pour method in Asia, early in paper's history. Making similar sheets rapidly is the main advantage of the dip method, so the dip hand mold came into greater use as demand for paper grew. Most papermakers used the dip method, including all hand papermakers in Europe and the United States. But some papermakers in Siam, Tibet, and other places kept on using the pour method.

This book deals mainly with the pour method. The equipment is easier to make, and a better piece of paper is made with less practice and experience. Also, a lot of pulp does not have to be prepared to make just one sheet. Regardless of what method you use, when you make a sheet of paper, you join a long continuous line of papermakers stretching back unbroken over 20 centuries. Exciting!

Hand Mold

The papermaker's chief tool has always been the hand mold. A hand mold is made of a sieve material, surrounded on its top edges by a fixed or movable rim, called a *deckle*. In the past, the hand mold has been made of different things and in different ways. After the first cloth/bamboo mold, changes were made. In Asia, the sieves became woven mats of reeds, grasses, or finely cut bamboo strips. The mats rested on wooden ribs in a frame. After the mold was dipped into a vat, the mat could be lifted from the frame for the next paper-making steps.

When wire was invented in Europe, in the middle of the fourteenth century, it was used instead of the reeds, grasses, and bamboo strips. Strung in strands from

He Saved Paper's History

Much of what we know about the history of papermaking is due to a man named Dard Hunter. During a visit to a London museum, young Hunter became fascinated with hand papermaking. A scholar and graphic artist, Hunter felt a great desire to know more about the history of paper, its production tools, the people who invented it, and its geographical trails. His interest became a lifelong study.

In travels prior to World War II, he scoured China, Japan, Korea, and all of Asia, sites of the earliest papermaking. Then he turned to Europe. In each place, he collected paper samples and implements. He also noted methods of manufacture. Everything Hunter found, he recorded in books. He made paper by hand, designed his own font, and hand-printed the books he wrote. Between these rare handmade books, several trade books, and his museum, Hunter cataloged 18 centuries of papermaking.

His museum was first housed at MIT and later at the Institute of Paper Chemistry (where I had the honor of serving as its curator for six years). It is now at the Georgia Institute of Technology in Atlanta, housed in the Robert C. Williams Museum of Papermaking.

Dard Hunter (on the right) with the author in 1964.

one side of a frame to the other, it became known as the *screen*. Around 1750, papermakers began to use woven wire for their molds. Instead of strands running in one direction, it was like the screen you now use to make your sheet (like the screen in a window). Papermakers changed to woven wire because they believed it gave paper a smoother surface for printing. Paper made on molds with wires running in just one direction is called *laid;* often you can see the impression of lines running across its surface. Paper made on molds with woven wire is called *wove.*

Early papermakers in the United States used both laid and wove molds. At first, they were all imported from Europe. Just before the Revolutionary War, Isaac Langle and Nathan Sellers started making them in the United States. Molds began to lose out when a Frenchman, Nicholas-Louis Robert invented a paper machine in 1798. It made paper faster than workers could do it by hand. Soon hand papermakers and mold makers alike had less and less work. Papermakers and mold makers in Europe dwindled to just a handful. In the United States, they disappeared altogether.

But for more than 1,500 years, every bit of paper used in the world was made by hand. Someone bent his or her back to dip every sheet. (To see what a modern hand mold looks like, *see page 53.*)

Deckle

The raised edge around the sieve of a mold, which keeps the water and fibers from running off the sides, is called the deckle. It is a part of every hand mold. In tin can papermaking (*see page 42*), the deckle is the small can you put on top of the screen. It not only keeps the water from running all over, it also determines the size and shape of the sheet. In methods using a standard mold and deckle, the finished sheet is rectangular. Want a different shape or size of paper? Use a different deckle.

In the pour method, the deckle can be quite high. In the dip method, deckles are shallow and may not rise more than ¼″ around the edges of the sieve. Whenever we speak of a hand mold, we are talking about some type of a sieve or screen material with a deckle around it. (For information on a modern deckle, *see page 40*).

Fibers

Fibers from all kinds of plants have been used for papermaking. Sometimes, in the past, papermakers got their fibers directly from plants. At other times, fibers were taken from old cloth, rope, or other things plants had been made into. For many years in Europe and the United States, only rags were used by papermakers. They didn't know how to get fibers from anything else. The rags were worn-out clothes made from linen (which came from flax plants) or cotton, also a plant product.

If you read a newspaper in colonial days, you might have seen want ads placed by papermakers offering to buy rags. You might have received three pennies a pound for them. In those days, three pennies bought much more than they do today. Benjamin Franklin was one of the rag buyers and sellers. He helped start a number of paper mills.

Because there were not enough rags in the colonies, they were imported from England, Germany, Italy, Egypt, and other countries. One papermaker said he could tell which country the rags came from by how clean they were. Rags played such an important part in paper manufacture, a little poem was made up about them (*below*). People still prize "rag content" paper today.

an old papermaking saying:

**rags make paper,
paper makes money,
money makes banks,
banks make loans,
loans make beggars,
beggars make rags.**

Rags to Wood

When did European and American paper-makers switch from rags to wood and other plants for making paper? Around 1850. Why? Because there weren't enough rags to make all the paper people wanted. That made scientists look for an alternate base for papermaking. Papermakers in the Eastern world were already making paper from plants, but papermakers in the Western world didn't know about it.

Scientists in Europe and the United States worked hard, trying many different plants. They even made experimental paper from things like algae and cow dung. Soon, paper was being made from straw. Eventually, paper was made by reducing trees to chips that were then cooked in chemicals. Trees are more or less big bundles of fibers. Papermakers have not had trouble with a shortage of fibers since.

Besides rags and plants, fibers have always been available from used paper. All paper is fiber. When paper is through being used for a letter or anything else, the fibers are still good. Fibers in paper can be taken apart much more easily than those in trees and used again.

Wasp Wisdom

While papermaking scientists were searching for a fiber source to replace rags, the humble wasp already had the answer. For centuries, it had been making paper — very *good* paper. It was the wasp's house, and it had to withstand rain, hail, wind, freezing temperatures, and thawing. And every fiber used was not from rags, but from trees. If people could make paper from trees, there would never be a fiber shortage.

In 1719, a French naturalist named René-Antoine de Réaumur laid a report before the French Royal Academy of Sciences which read, "They (wasps) teach us that paper can be made from fibers of plants without the use of rags and linen, and seem to invite us to try whether we can make fine and good paper from the use of certain woods." In 1765, Dr. Jacob Christian Schäffer, a German naturalist, read the report and proceeded to make paper in the laboratory from plants and wasp's nests, adding 25 percent cotton fiber.

You, too, can make wasp nest paper. Find an abandoned — repeat, *abandoned* — nest. Usually, a nest is reliably abandoned following a deep freeze. To be safe, collect a nest in freezing weather, seal it in plastic, and keep it in your freezer for a while. After thawing it out, recycle it in a blender as described for any other fiber (*see page 4*). Recycling affects the wasp's fiber, though, and your sheet might be weak. If so, either make a thicker sheet or add a percentage of brown grocery sack fibers.

And so we salute the noble wasp. When humans were still scratching on cave walls, the wasp had been making paper for centuries. However, it might be best to send our salute by e-mail rather than by making contact personally.

Recycled Paper Is Not New

Probably no current product has been recycled longer than paper has — for more than 14 centuries. Evidence indicates the Chinese, who invented it, recycled paper in the fourth and fifth centuries. Paper recycling, to varying degrees, has continued ever since. It probably increased whenever a shortage of raw materials occurred and decreased when raw materials were plentiful and inexpensive.

In the Western world, from the twelfth to the mid-nineteenth centuries, all paper was made with recycled fibers. The respected cotton and linen rag papers of old were 100 percent recycled cotton and/or linen rags. Machines literally beat the rags back down to the individual cotton or linen fibers that made up the threads. No other industry has existed so long on 100 percent recycling.

In this book, "recycling" means taking paper (which is essentially a batch of dry fibers), turning it into individual fibers with water and a blender, and making them back into handmade paper. This book seeks to open your mind and eyes to the vast store of valuable papermaking components lying idle in the world's stores of wastepaper. To think of these fibers as "used" would be like thinking of a new car driven home from a dealer's showroom as "used" and then throwing it away. A simple fact needs recognition: Wastepaper is not waste fiber.

The paper industry's finest treasures (not only fibers, but additives and color from dyes) are in wastepaper piles and available to hand papermakers absolutely free. The beautiful three- or four-color handmade sheet that can be made in four minutes by recycling would take days, money, and equipment to make if the papermaker started with new white pulp.

Every different type of paper you recycle gives you a different kind of handmade sheet. This happens because there is a difference between *pulp* and *furnish*. Pulp is simply fibers. Furnish is fibers plus additives. Furnish is a recipe of fibers, sizing, fillers, optical brighteners, and so forth. Not much paper is made of just fibers.

Industry spends a lot of time, money, and research, plus testing and evaluating, to arrive at the right furnish. When they use new fibers, they have to find, buy, and properly add all the necessary additives. When you recycle, all the additives have already been selected, added, and paid for. For you, it's free and only as far away as your wastebasket. By recycling, you can make handmade paper with every furnish ever created by the paper industry. Each different sheet you recycle produces a different (slightly or radically) handmade sheet.

Wastepaper is considered waste because it cannot be used again as paper, but the *fibers* are not waste. Their useful life has hardly started. Not only is wastepaper not waste fiber, but science shows that for some paper qualities, recycled fibers are superior to new fibers. They have been studied in hundreds of research projects, and the paper industry is relentless in its quest to use higher percentages of recycled fibers.

What Can Be Recycled?

All and any paper can be recycled. If it can't be recycled, it isn't paper. Recycle everything to find out what it is you like to recycle. Just like new fibers, recyclable fibers run the gamut from cheap to the world's finest. At the bottom of quality and cost are groundwood fibers, amply available as newsprint. At the top of the line are cotton and certain wood fibers pulped by advanced pulping technology, bleached for whiteness and/or further purification, and perhaps in a furnish, including opacifiers and optical brighteners. Here's a bit of information about commonly available papers:

Newsprint. With newsprint you can make handmade paper that might contain a recycled comic strip (a big hit with kids) or a newspaper story about friends. Its short fibers are good for watermarking. Newsprint makes a nice gray sheet. One disadvantage is that the ink released from the fibers makes a rather dirty film or scum that gets on the papermaking equipment

A Very Special Place

The Paper Discovery Center in Appleton, Wisconsin, is a very busy place. This hands-on museum celebrates all things paper, with a particular focus on the environmental aspects of modern papermaking. Visitors learn about the management of clean water for rivers, and about forest management to replace trees and foster wildlife habitat. More than 50 percent of the fiber used in the industry is recycled.

Four thousand students a year participate in a paper science curriculum, and more than 300 Scouts have earned merit badges in papermaking. And every one of the center's 36,000 visitors, regardless of age, makes paper by recycling with an Arnold Grummer pour handmold. David Lee, the director, says that the Center's goals are to energize an interest in science through the understanding of paper. Enthusiasm runs high, captured perfectly by a young visitor who told his parents, "Do I want to come back here again? Yeah, a thousand times!"

Tell the advertiser - "I found you in the AT&T Yellow Pages"

HotSpring Portable Spas

We also offer: SOLANA HOT SPOT TIGER RIVER SPAS

Serving Northeast Wisconsin for Over 24 Years

Our Place. Your Space.℠

Hot-Hotels 315

• World's #1 selling brand
• Easy to own and operate
• Consumers Digest® rated the Tiger
• Consumers Digest®
• Exclusive features
• Extremely energy

"For ex

and can turn white papermaking screens gray. Avoid the ink problem by cutting off and using only the unprinted margins. Always clean all the equipment thoroughly after each use.

Home or business paper.

This covers a broad spectrum of good-looking, highly acceptable fibers in good furnishes. They offer colors, as well as shades of white. Hold sheets to light to see if a watermark tells you the cotton content. Avoid printed ink effects by cutting away and using only the unprinted areas. Or use the inked sections to give a visual texture and color to handmade sheets.

Envelopes.
These can be the backbone of white pulp supply. They are generally clean and range into the highest whiteness and the best fibers. They offer a wide range of colored fibers. Color from ink is bountiful from "security" envelopes where the inside of the envelope is printed with a colored pattern. Discard the glued flaps. Large envelopes often offer long fibers for strength. For pure white or colored pulp, use only the unprinted areas.

Bags.
Many bags offer long fibers for strength. Custom bags from upscale department stores can offer great and unusual colors. Plain brown sacks offer a great natural earth-tone background for some botanicals. White grocery bags are the result of very expensive long-fiber, bleached pulp. A short presoak before blending helps but is not necessary. The long fibers tend to "flock" (*see* Defining Terms, *pages 28–29*) in handmade sheets.

Wrapping papers.
These are a happy hunting ground for colors, unusual inks, and foils. Including them in the mix will result in dramatic mottling.

Magazines.
Slick and shiny pages of any publication can be recycled. The fiber quality varies. Magazine covers offer unusual possibilities for handmade sheets.

Colored papers.
These are dyed fibers and therefore a source of colored pulp for colored handmade papers. Because of poor fiber and dyes that run, avoid "construction" paper when recycling.

Superlative fibers.
For superlative fibers, look for superlative uses. The paper used for programs (for concerts, drama, opera, etc.) is likely to be very high

quality. The same is usually true of invitations to landmark events, anniversary programs, and publications from financial institutions.

Christmas papers.

Harvest colored envelopes for dyed fibers; cards with lots of metallic ink; Christmas wrapping paper with color, heavy ink, or foil components; illustrations from cards to be surface embedded on next year's cards; ribbons, strings, and more for inclusion in next year's cards.

Frequently Asked Questions

Q: I made a large art piece from recycled paper and noticed some of the colors have faded. Any suggestions?

A: Light is probably the most prominent cause of fading. Direct sunshine is a prime threat; so is continuous and prolonged exposure to incandescent and fluorescent light. Cheap papers having residual lignin (groundwood newsprint) fade the most and fastest. Cheap dyes (as in much construction paper) will bring fast fading. Lignin-free and colorfast papers may be candidates for recycling to lessen fading.

For prized papers, use common sense. Avoid long exposure to sunlight, bright room lighting, and continually changing temperature and relative humidity. Hang framed paper art at wall locations featuring mostly ambient light. Filters and safer light sources (special bulbs or fluorescent tubes) are available. Consultation with a paper conservator will be of value.

Recycled papers come from all kinds of stuff . . .

Hamburger wrappers

Sunday funnies

Sales circulars

Labels from
cans and jars

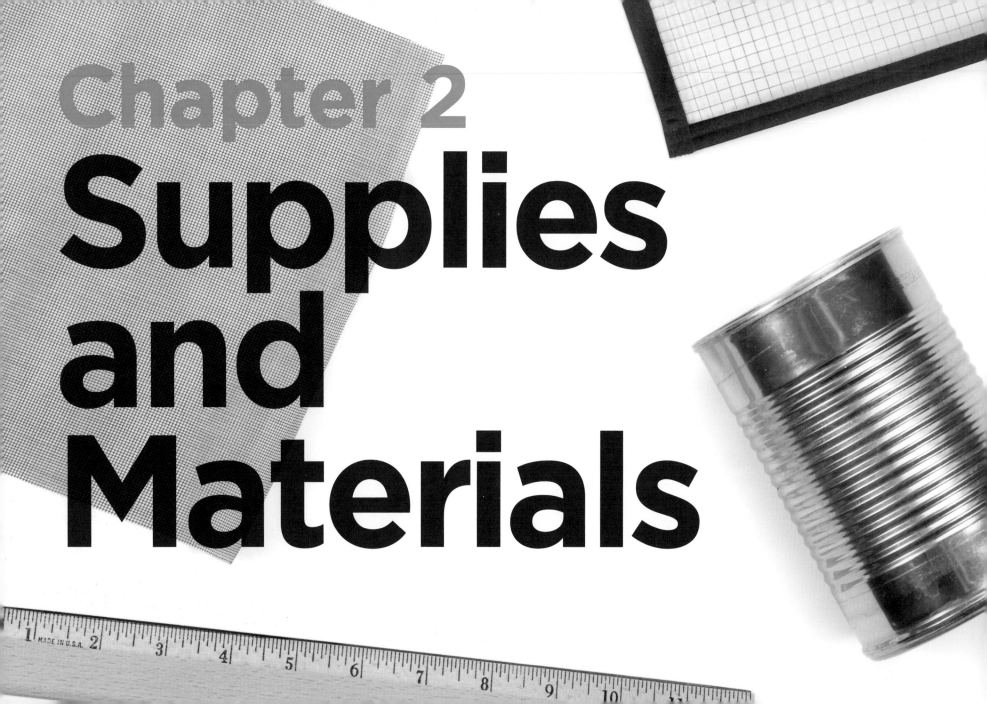

Chapter 2
Supplies and Materials

Most of the supplies you need to make paper, with the exception of a mold, deckle, or press, are already in your kitchen. In the case of tin can papermaking, however, you can construct a mold and deckle for free from a few recycled tin cans. The only other things you need are curiosity, willingness to experiment, and a basic understanding of how paper is made. Read on!

Gathering Your Supplies

Paper is one of the easiest waste products to recycle. The possibilities for creating one-of-a-kind recycled paper are right there in your home recycling bin — newspapers, magazines, junk mail, coupons, and grocery store flyers. Collect some labels from bottles and cans, old letters and envelopes, concert or theater programs and tickets, flyers and pamphlets, and you have a breadth of choice that is beyond comprehension!

Papermaking can be done at home or in a classroom, in just about any place where you have sources for water and power nearby. A kitchen counter is great, so you don't have to worry about water spattering around. The following list of basics will get you started. Or, if you prefer, you can purchase ready-to-use kits or individual items such as papermaking screens at many craft stores. Some kits contain everything except the vat, tray, iron, and blender (see Resources, page 196).

Blender. This basic item is what you'll use for preparing pulp slurry. Any kitchen blender will do; the more basic, the better. It's best to have a blender you can devote exclusively to papermaking, unless you want to spend a lot of time scrubbing out all the pieces after each use. So, if you don't have a spare blender already, you might want to pick up one at a yard sale or secondhand shop.

Molds and deckles. We'll talk about molds in detail in the next chapter and even tell you how to make your own (see page 50). If you want to try tin can papermaking, all you need are two containers: one large one on the bottom to catch the water runoff and one of equal size or smaller for the top (see page 42 for details).

Vat. For home papermaking, all you need is a dishpan large enough to accommodate the hand mold.

Drain pan. This can be a tray, cookie sheet, or similar item with sides to catch the water.

Screens. These will be explained later in detail, but essentially, you will need fine nonmetallic mesh for the papermaking screen, to catch the fibers while allowing the water to drain. You also will need a stiffer support screen, which may or may not be attached to a frame that can double as a drain rack. A selection of screens can be found in local craft supply or hardware stores.

Sponge. A couple of good cellulose sponges that fit your hand and are easy to grab are useful for soaking up excess water on your new sheet of paper.

Couch sheets. For pressing and drying your sheets, you can use thick paper toweling, blotter sheets, or other absorbent material in pieces larger than the sheet of paper being made (see page 26).

Press bar. Used to press out water, this can be any piece of flat metal, wood, or plastic, or a book encased in a plastic zip-top bag.

Iron. An iron comes in handy for drying paper quickly. You just need one with a basic, high-heat setting. Be sure the steam is turned off!

Pulp gun. Any container, such as a turkey baster or mustard bottle, can be used to dispense pulp (see page 27).

Pressing equipment. There are a number of creative ways to press your paper (see page 27). You don't need a full-blown press. However, if you're really interested in pursuing papermaking, we provide instructions for making your own press (see page 34).

Frequently Asked Questions

Q: What kind of blender is best for papermaking?

A: No type of special blender is needed to recycle paper; however, V-shape blenders that are narrower at the bottom (where the blade is) are more efficient. The paper can't stay away from the blade as it can with U-shape blenders that are wide at the bottom. Often, the older the blender, the more sturdy it is, although some old blenders do have weak motors. "Bells and whistles" are not necessary. The fewer speeds a blender has, the better. Actually, a single-speed blender is as good as a 15-speed, and usually less expensive. Presoaking paper can help poor blenders.

Q: Do I need a paper press?

A: Stacking weights on top of newly formed sheets makes paper dry smoothly. For this reason, many papermakers use pressure for drying. A press can apply more pressure than weights can. It is especially good for paper that has had something transplanted to its surface. Paper dried under a lot of pressure has flat and smooth edges. Its surface is also smoother than paper dried under little pressure.

When paper was made by hand, paper mills had huge presses built especially for them. Today, hand papermakers sometimes can find old presses used by other trades, such as printing and bookbinding. But the easiest and cheapest way to get a press is to build one. With a small jack, like those used for changing tires on cars, you can build an economical press (*see page 34*).

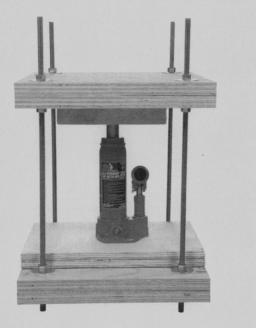

I designed this do-it-yourself, 2-ton hydraulic press especially for hand papermakers.

Couching Materials

In papermaking, *couching* means taking the new wet sheet off the papermaking screen. Too weak to be lifted off by hand, the sheet must be coaxed off with the aid of absorbent material called a *couch sheet*, which acts like a blotter. In the past, felts of a special wool and weave were used in hand papermaking mills. These are no longer available, nor is the training on how to use them. You can use any stable material that is absorbent, including thick paper towels or cloth.

Blotter paper is perhaps the most efficient, easiest, and surest material to work. It is inexpensive and can be dried and reused. Precut professional papermakers' blotter couch sheets also are available (*see Resources, page 196*). General desk blotters might be found at office supply stores. These will have to be cut and might not be as satisfactory for papermaking. If colored, they might bleed onto wet sheets. Interestingly, new sheets can be couched off the screen onto almost any solid surface, as shown in board drying on page 114.

Pulp Guns

A pulp gun is vital in making art and decoration with fibers. In this book, a pulp gun is any container from which pulp slurry can be squirted (shot), poured, or shaken in bursts or in a sprinkle. A **turkey baster** is a good choice, as are plastic containers with spouts or nozzles, such as **mustard dispensers, plastic cosmetic containers, plastic shaving lotion bottles, syrup or honey dispensers, and plastic laboratory bottles** with spouts that can be snipped off for smaller or larger openings. Another easily made solution is a **plastic soda bottle** with a hole drilled in the cap.

Keep your eyes open for any kind of dispensing container and try it. Different effects can be produced by varying the thickness of the pulp slurries, the squirting force, and the angle at which the pulp is shot into or onto pulp or onto a bare screen (*see chapter 5*).

Pressing Equipment

Pressing handmade paper is simply a matter of applying pressure to sheets to remove water. This process can be simple and inexpensive or more complicated and very expensive. The method doesn't have much effect on the final result, as long as it's done right. But the more pressure that is applied, the more some sheet characteristics are enhanced.

Simple. After placing the wet sheet of paper between couching materials, add weight, such as a stack of books, concrete or stone building blocks, or pieces of metal.

Expensive. Commercial presses can range from a two-ton, easily portable, screw press with a price around $300, to hydraulic presses costing $3,000 or more. Watch for presses made for other purposes that also can be used for paper. A prime example is the coveted and now costly bookbinder's press.

Another option is to build your own drying press. See the instructions on page 34, which show an easily built, inexpensive press frame. It uses a two-ton hydraulic auto jack available from any discount store. It works beautifully.

People, Pressure, and Paper

What's the difference between people and paper? People don't like pressure; paper does.

What the press is particularly good for — besides sheet hardening, stabilization, and causing more internal bonding area — is getting botanicals into or onto sheets, as well as embedment of various things in or on sheet surfaces.

Less pressure limits the papermaker to mostly smaller, flat, flexible botanicals, such as individual flower petals, leaves, segments of delicate stems, ferns, blades of grass, and other flat and thin items. With two tons of pressure, I'm tempted to say you can throw in most anything: whole blooms, barley beards, bulky stem segments, the works. (Don't try a whole sapling!)

Nothing can make a multi-element sheet into a cohesive whole the way a couple hours of continuous two-ton pressure will do. Can you make good paper without it? Certainly, but the press lets you climb a bit higher on the ladder.

defining papermaking terms

It seems every vocation has a list of words with meanings specific to that endeavor. Papermaking is no exception. Read through this glossary and refer back to it if you run across an unfamiliar term while completing one of the projects.

casting

Making a copy of a form or dimensional surface by applying wet pulp, then letting the pulp dry.

couch (say it: "koosh")

To remove a newly formed paper sheet (wet mat of fibers) from a papermaking screen. Too weak to be lifted off by hand, the new sheet is placed against a flat surface to which it will transfer when pressure is applied.

couch materials

Any materials with a surface that will cause a new sheet to transfer from a papermaking screen when the new sheet is pressed against it.

couch sheet

In papermaking, a reusable blotter sheet made especially for couching new sheets from papermaking screens.

cover screen

A piece of window screen or other suitable material laid over a newly formed paper sheet to protect the sheet during water removal with a sponge.

curl and cockle

The result of uneven shrinkage when a sheet of paper is not dried uniformly, such as when using an iron. Uneven drying means uneven shrinkage, pulling different parts of the sheet in different directions, causing either general curl or localized cockling, or both.

deckle

The removable top part of a hand mold. The deckle sits on or fits around the papermaking screen and prevents pulp from running off the screen. Because it creates the outer limits to which pulp can flow on the screen, the deckle determines the sheet's shape and size.

drain pan

Any tray, cookie pan, or similar container on which to lay a papermaking screen and newly formed sheet for initial water removal.

drain rack

Any gridlike structure placed in the drain pan upon which a screen and newly formed sheet can be placed to facilitate water drainage from the sheet. In some kits, the hand mold's screen support also serves as the drain rack.

dry lap

Dry pulp in sheet form.

fiber

Cellulose strands produced by a plant. It will bond naturally to other cellulose fibers when it touches them in water. Also sometimes used as a synonym for pulp.

flock

A tendency of fibers to gather in bunches during sheet formation, instead of dispersing evenly as individuals. Flocking is visible when a sheet is held up to light.

furnish

Pulp that consists of fibers plus all additives (sizing, opacifiers, fillers, etc.) required to make a specific type of paper.

hand mold

A device for making paper by hand. It consists of a screen, screen support, and a deckle.

pulp

The raw material for making paper. It consists of individual fibers. Dry pulp is generally a sheet of fibers called "dry lap." Wet pulp is fibers in water. Papermakers generally begin with fibers in dry form.

release agent

A substance applied to a surface or form before wet pulp is applied in making a casting. When the pulp has dried, its removal from the surface or form is eased by the release agent.

screen

Material woven or formed into a sievelike fabric which will let water flow through but trap papermaking fibers on its surface. Previously, strands woven or laid side-by-side were primarily metal. Today, screens are primarily specially formulated plastic.

slurry

In this book, water with fibers in it.

vat

A container into which pulp is placed when a dip mold is used, and into which water is placed when a pour mold is used. The vat must be large enough to accommodate the hand mold and the papermaker's hands simultaneously.

Where to Find Pulp

Once you've collected your supplies, you will of course need some pulp. One of the great benefits of making recycled paper is that almost every type of pulp is instantly available at the mere whirl of a blender. There's a treasure trove of free fiber just sitting in the recycling bin! Recycling is by far the simplest and most accessible means of obtaining pulp.

If you wish, though, you can find other sources for pulp fibers. Today's "start from scratch" papermakers are experimenting with fibers from many traditional and new plants. Traditional ones include Asian plants, such as gampi, mitsumata, and kozo, whose fibers require special formation aids and sheet forming techniques. Also traditional are hemp, abaca, and cotton rag. The easiest pulp to use and obtain is cotton linter (*see page 125*), available in convenient packages at art and craft stores and from papermaking suppliers (*see* Resources, *page 196*).

Wood fibers are most readily available to hand papermakers by recycling. Though tested by the commercial paper industry years ago, abaca (banana plant fiber) is gaining popularity with hand papermakers. A variety of special pulps are available from papermaking suppliers (*see* Resources). Some are produced from discarded fabrics. White cotton rag pulp may have formerly been bed sheets, and blue denim pulp was likely blue jean material. Discarded T-shirts are sorted by hue to make brightly colored pulps. Linen pulp might have been a tablecloth or article of clothing. Specialty pulps might include some synthetic and cellulose fiber blends. These pulps will make waterleaf (blotter) paper unless sizing is added (*see page 33*).

About the Additives

When preparing the pulp, a paper mill almost always adds something to the fibers to make the end paper have desirable qualities, depending on how it's going to be used. There are hundreds of additives that will make the paper brighter, bulkier, colorful, water-resistant, fire-retardant, able to hold ink without feathering, or whatever fits the desired use. Each additive costs money and time to insert into the pulp, and often requires special equipment, as well as specialized knowledge and expertise.

But the home papermaker who recycles gets all of this for free, in practically no time: the fibers (refined or unrefined), additives, cost of equipment, and cost of salaries of professional and scientific personnel required to assemble the pulp. Whether your dream is to create paper that is wild and exotic or tame and standard, single color or multicolored, smooth or textured, recycling offers the chance to fulfill this dream. Experiment and you'll be amazed by the magical trash-to-treasure paper transformation you can make right in your kitchen.

recycling is the simplest means of obtaining pulp

Where to Find Pulp
(the easy answer)

1. Tear up paper and put it in a blender with water.

2. Run the blender for 30 seconds or less, turning the paper into pulp.

how much paper?
how much water?
see page 48.

Making Paper That Will Last

There are, of course, no circumstances under which any paper is permanent. Regardless of how permanent or archival a paper is said to be:

O a single spark can obliterate it

O a serious heat surge nearby can damage it

O light can age it

O water can dissolve it

O cars passing your open window can reduce its longevity

O insects in your house can eat it

O mold and fungi can grow on it

All of the above paper predators don't give two hoots as to whether paper is said to be permanent, archival, or pure groundwood (lignin-loaded). So the first thing to understand is that the frame of reference for these terms is relative.

For keeping memories, papers offer more hope of longevity if they are acid-free (i.e., permanent or archival). Essentially, this means the pH level, which is a measurable quality, is in the immediate vicinity of 7.5. Readings lower than 7.0 are acidic; those with higher readings are alkaline. Papermaking conditions that would normally lead to an acidic reading (below 7.0 pH) can be treated by adding an acid buffer to the pulp. The buffer, usually calcium carbonate, also will provide protection from possible acid contamination after the sheet is made.

But note this: Even if you have never heard of acid-free, permanence, archival, or lignin, the paper you make is not going to fall apart tomorrow, next week, or even probably for years. Indeed, much of such paper will outlast the people who made it.

How to Make Memories-Safe Paper

Can you make your handmade paper safe for memories? Yes. It helps to have a pH testing pen or tape to keep track of the pH of your paper and the paper you are planning to recycle. Here are three methods for making your paper last.

Method 1. Using recycled or new pulp, make paper as you always do. When the paper is dry, spray it with a commercial buffering solution. Your paper is then within the pH range usually ascribed to permanent or archival paper. Solutions are available from archival catalogs and papermaking suppliers (*see* Resources, *page 196*).

Method 2. When using recycled paper or new pulp that is not acid-free, add calcium carbonate to the pulp, in the blender or in the vat. Make sure that your supplier includes directions with the calcium carbonate and follow them exactly. Calcium carbonate will automatically adjust your papermaking system to the correct pH level.

Method 3. Buy acid-free pulp. But then make sure your water, couch sheets or felts, and any additives are all acid-free (ask suppliers about the pH of their products). You can use distilled water, which is generally not in the acidic pH range.

What Is Sizing?

Sizing helps fibers (individually or as a paper structure) resist moisture and liquids. If not sized, fibers and the paper made with them are hydrophilic, like sponges and blotters. Try to write or draw on them with ink, and the ink will run and go fuzzy.

When recycling, some of the paper you use may already have sizing in it. How do you know? Try writing on it with a felt-tip pen and see if the ink spreads. Or place a small drop of water on the surface of a sheet; the longer it takes the drop to absorb into the sheet, the better the sizing.

Fibers can be sized individually as part of the pulp before the sheet is made (*internal* sizing), or en masse as a formed sheet (*external* sizing). Sizing can be soft (adding just a bit of moisture resistance), hard, or somewhere between. In the commercial paper industry, sizing is costly and is therefore introduced into paper in just the amount the paper's use demands. It is not a simple process, because when put into pulp, most of it washes off the fibers during water drainage. To prevent this, scientists add a second agent that chemically bonds the sizing to the fibers.

Fortunately, there are simpler ways for you to size your paper (*see* How to Size Your Handmade Paper, *below*). Sources for commercial sizing are listed in Resources.

How to Size Your Handmade Paper

There are a number of products you can use to size your paper, available through paper suppliers. The most commonly found sizing materials are wax, starch, and gelatin. No matter which you use, always follow the manufacturer's instructions on the labels.

Wax makes excellent sizing and is easy to use, effective, and easy to get for free. To make your own, collect some waxed paper sacks (they look and feel waxy), like the ones bakeries use to send pastries home with customers. To reuse the wax for sizing, here's what you do:

1. Tear up the waxed sack and soak it in hot water for 15 minutes. You also can use waxed paper, but it's a little harder to pulp in the blender.

2. Run the soaked pieces in a blender with hot water. For a waxed sack equal to ¾ of an 8½″ × 11″ sheet of paper, use 2½ to 3 cups of water. Run the blender until there are no paper chunks visible.

Now you have about 3 cups of excellent liquid sizing. Using it is easy. Put some into the pulp (when using a pour mold) or into the vat (when using a dip mold) and mix well. You can use a little or a lot.

- For soft sizing, add one part waxed sack pulp to five parts general recycled pulp.

- For hard sizing, add equal parts waxed sack pulp and general recycled pulp.

- For even harder sizing, add three parts waxed sack pulp to one part general recycled pulp.

- For new pulp, and especially cotton pulp (rag or linters), sizing will be a bit softer. The more pure a fiber, the harder it is to size.

Building a Paper Press

In this home-built press, the platforms are held in place on rods with washers and nuts. Pressure is applied by pumping the hydraulic jack up against the top platform, which holds wet sheets absolutely flat while they dry. The press built in this project is big enough for up to 8″ × 12″ sheets of paper. If you are not accustomed to working with power tools, ask someone experienced to help you.

Instructions

1. Glue 2 of the plywood pieces together, making a platform 1½″ thick. Clamp the pieces together or put weights on them until the glue has dried. Do the same with the other 2 plywood pieces. (The platforms will last longer if you put a waterproof paint or varnish on them.)

(CONTINUED ON PAGE 36)

Materials

- O Wood glue **A**
- O Four pieces of ¾″ plywood, 1 foot square **B**
- O Two wood clamps or weights **C**
- O Waterproof paint or varnish (optional)
- O Pencil **D**
- O Drill and ⅜″, ¹³⁄₃₂″, ⁷⁄₁₆″, and 1″ bits **E**
- O Two threaded rods, ⅜″ diameter and 36″ long **F**
- O Hacksaw **G**
- O 16 nuts, ⅜″ **H**
- O 16 washers, 1½″ wide with ⅜″ hole **I**
- O 2-ton hydraulic jack **J**
- O One 6″ length of 2″ × 4″ lumber **K**
- O Two 8″ × 12″ boards **L**
- O Ruler **K**

Upsizing

You can use this press for any 5½″ x 8½″ sheets made with the molds featured in this book, as well as any papers you make with the Tin Can Papermaking method. If you make paper sheets larger than 8″ x 12″, however, you will need a larger press. Adapt the design by using plywood pieces that are at least 4″ larger than the paper you want to press.

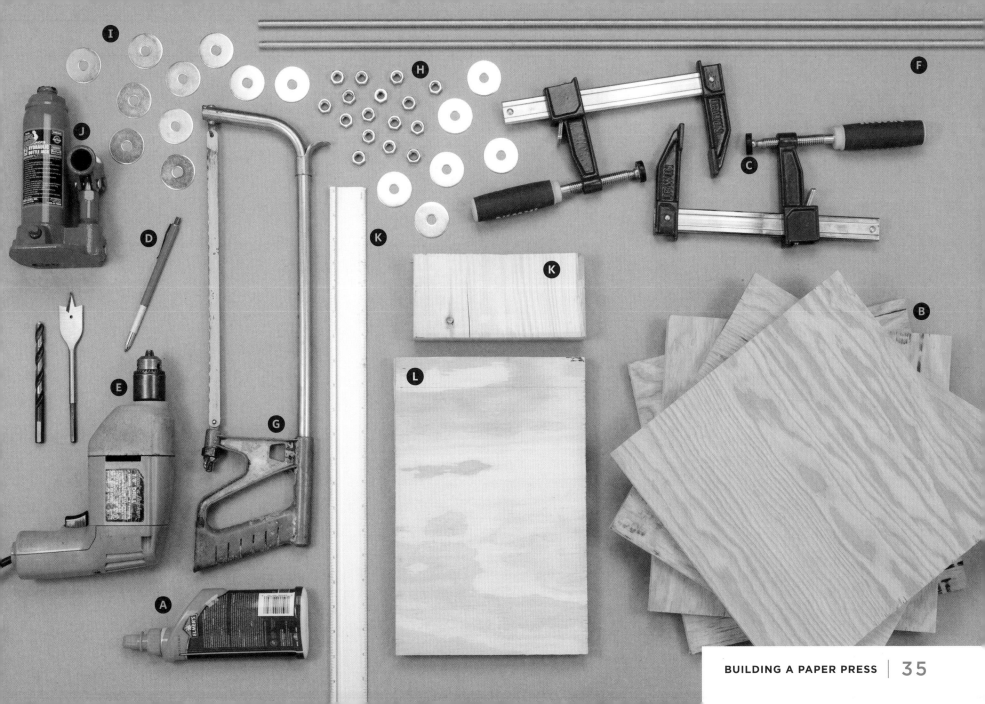

2. Draw a line across each platform 1½" in from each edge. Where the lines cross at each corner, drill a ⅜" hole.

3. Cut the 2 threaded rods in half, making 4 threaded rods, each 18" long.

4. Assemble the platforms on both ends of the 4 rods with a nut and washer above and below each of the 4 rods as shown. If it is difficult to thread the rods through the holes, drill the holes again with a ¹³⁄₃₂" or ⁷⁄₁₆" drill bit.

5. The top of the jack's piston is small, and the pressure it puts against the press's top platform must be distributed over a greater area. To address this, measure to find the center of the 6" length of 2" × 4" lumber, and drill a 1" hole that is about ⅜" deep. Insert the tip of the piston into the hole. This will put the block of wood between piston top and the bottom of the press's top platform.

Opposite: Place paper and couch sheets between the 8" × 12" boards to press papers flat.

Couch sheets and paper are between these boards

Using the Paper Press

1. When a sheet has been couched from the screen, remove enough water so it can be lifted from the couch sheet. Place the wet sheet between dry couch sheets and put them between two 8″ × 12″ boards.

2. Place the boards on the bottom platform of the press and set the jack on top of the boards.

3. Pump the jack's piston up against the bottom of the top platform. If the piston does not reach the top platform, put more boards under the jack. Apply pressure for 10 to 15 minutes. To keep water from running back into the sheet when the pressure is released, brush the edges of the pressing boards with a damp sponge.

4. Release the jack. Replace the damp couch sheets with dry ones, and put the papers back into the press. Apply pressure for 1 to 2 hours.

5. Change the couch sheets. Apply pressure for about 3 hours (overnight is good).

6. Continue changing couch sheets until the paper is dry. The thicker the paper, the more changes will be required.

Chapter 3
Easy Papermaking Techniques

If you're ready to jump in and make paper, using items you already have in your kitchen, tin can papermaking is for you! **Simply rescue a few tin cans, plastic bottles, and other containers from the trash, pull out a blender, and you've got what you need to start making your own recycled paper. Also covered in this chapter is a super-easy way to make paper with a pour mold. All you need are curiosity and a willingness to experiment. You'll have a stack of handmade paper in no time!**

Pour vs. Dip

The first sheet of paper was likely made with a **pour** hand mold. In this method of papermaking, a mold is placed in a vat of water and pulp is poured into the mold only, not into the vat. Another way to make paper is by using the **dip** method, which involves dipping a mold into a vat that contains pulp. The dip method was the only method used by European and American papermakers of the past and is considered the more traditional way to make paper.

For home papermaking, I've found the pour method to be the better way to go. The pour mold generally has higher deckle walls than a dip mold and can move easily from one type or color of sheet to another. A pour mold requires less preparation and cleanup than a dip mold and can make sheets not practical for a dip mold. Consequently, this method tends to be more versatile. I believe that anyone capable of lifting a pour mold out of water and holding it level while water drains will make a near-perfect sheet the first time he or she tries, regardless of age, handicap, intellectual level, or aptitude for "art." For these reasons, the primary focus of this book is the pour method. However, since many readers may already be using the dip method, I've included information for that method as well.

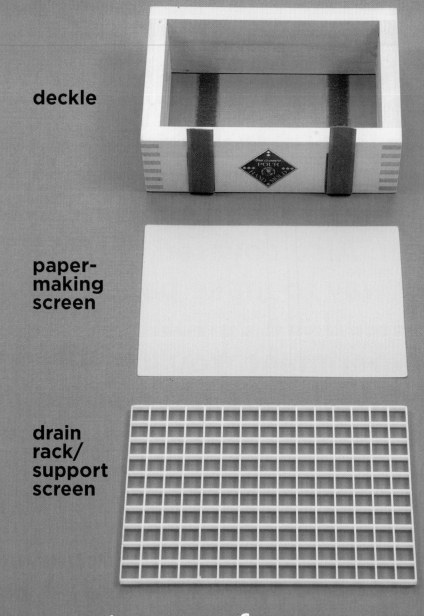

deckle

paper-making screen

drain rack/ support screen

anatomy of a pour mold

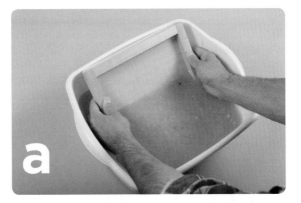

If Using a Dip Hand Mold

In a traditional dip mold, the top deckle is only about ¾" high, to allow pulp to more easily flow into the mold from the vat. The bottom support screen has a finer mesh, which serves as the papermaking screen. For my dip hand molds, I use the same support screen and papermaking screen as is used for the pour hand mold.

The procedure is basically the same as for pour hand molds (*see page 52*), but here are a couple of extra tips. After assembling your mold and preparing your pulp, here are the next steps:

Using modern materials, I designed a simplified dip hand mold that uses the same papermaking and support screens as the pour hand mold.

○ Select a vat large enough to accommodate the dip hand mold and your hands on each side. Pour prepared pulp into the vat until it is deep enough for the hand mold to be dipped totally beneath the pulp's surface. Actually, deeper is better.

○ Grasp both sides of the hand mold and dip it into the pulp vertically. Turn the hand mold slowly to a horizontal position against the vat's bottom, then lift it up and out of the pulp.

○ Remove the deckle from the screen. Couch the sheet off the screen, press it, and let it dry. Repeat. Note the thickness of each sheet. When the sheets get too thin, add more pulp to the vat. With very small vats, this can be after every two or three sheets.

Tin Can Paper-making

This technique, a variation on the pour method, is the simplest and cheapest way to start making your own paper at home. The basic supplies for tin can papermaking are pretty much the same as for regular handmade paper, with just a couple of modifications. The paper you make will be round, unless you experiment with other shaped containers to put on top of your screen. What can you do with round paper? You might be surprised by the variety of projects you'll find in chapter 8.

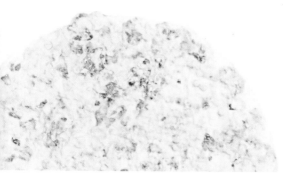

Gathering Your Supplies

As listed on page 25, you'll need a blender, drain pan, sponge, paper towels, a pressing board, and a clothes iron. The rest of what you will need:

Mold and deckle options.

Select two containers: one large one for the bottom to catch the water runoff, and one of equal size or smaller for the top. These can be tin cans, juice containers, milk jugs, or handmade molds (*see page 80*). The top container will serve as the deckle and should have both ends cut out. Whatever its size and shape, that's what your paper will be.

Papermaking screen.

A nonmetal piece of fine-mesh window screen, available inexpensively at hardware stores, makes a good papermaking screen. You'll need at least two 6" squares, or larger if your top container is larger. Window screen is right on the edge of being too coarse for papermaking, but most of the time it will work. Later, you might want to experiment with other "sieves," such as stiff pellon or coarse cloth.

Support screen. The support

screen can have larger holes and needs to be quite rigid, since your papermaking screen will rest on top of it. Plastic needlework canvas works well and is available in craft and fabric stores. Hardware cloth, made from metal, is available at hardware stores. It comes in a variety of mesh sizes, and any of them will work fine. After cutting it to size, wrap duct tape around any sharp edges before using, so no one gets cut. A 6" square support screen is a good size for most food and beverage cans. Larger sizes are necessary for larger diameter cans.

Containers. A measuring cup will help

you control the amount of water you use, and you'll need a couple of containers (such as tall plastic cups) for dividing up and pouring the pulp into the mold.

Tip

Any time you use a tin can for your mold, make sure to tape any sharp edges to prevent injury. For techniques that may involve reaching into the mold to manipulate the pulp, it's best to find a shorter can.

support screen

papermaking
screen

1,2

3a

3b

Step 1. Set a tin can, with one end cut out and facing up, into a drain pan. Over the open end, place a support screen, followed by a papermaking screen.

Step 2. Place a canister with both ends cut out over the window screen. If the cans are of the same size, match their rims. (The can on top can be smaller, but not larger, than the bottom can.) Presto! You have set up a "pour" hand mold with which you can make handmade paper.

Step 3. For a 4" to 5" diameter top can, pick a 7" square of waste or used paper, or smaller pieces of several papers that add up to a 7" square. Tear the paper into small pieces and put them in a blender. Add about 1½ cups water. Put on the lid and run the blender for 20 to 30 seconds.

Step 4. Pour half the blender's contents into each of two containers and add ½ cup water to each container.

Step 5. With a container in each hand, *dump* the contents of both containers at the same time into the top can. Pour from opposite sides so that streams from both containers hit each other. Let all water drain into the bottom can.

4

5

Why Pour from Two Cups?

The two-handed pour will likely distribute the fibers more evenly on the screen, giving you a nicer sheet. One-handed pouring can sometimes cause fibers to swirl around the outside edge of the can and make a donut sheet with a thin spot or hole in the middle. But you can give it a try: Simply pour the pulp into one container instead of two and add a cup of water. Hold the top can down with one hand and pour with the other.

Making Good Slurry

How much paper do you put in the blender? A general guideline is to put in a little more waste paper than it takes to cover the top can's opening. This will give you a handmade sheet about as thick as the waste paper you put in. The *more* waste paper you put in, the *thicker* the new sheet. The *less* waste paper you put in, the *thinner* the new sheet. (For more precise information, *see* Recycling Formulas for Pulp *on page 48.*)

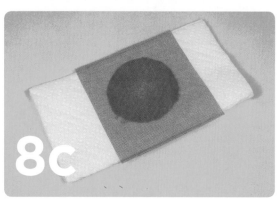

Step 6. Raise the top can straight up and off the screen. Lift both screens (with your new sheet of paper on it) and remove the tin can base. Place the screens back into the drain pan or onto a flat surface that is not harmed by water (such as a tabletop with several layers of cloth or a piece of plastic). Place another 6″ square piece of window screen over the new sheet.

Step 7. Take a dry sponge and press it down on top of the window screen and new sheet. Squeeze water from the sponge. Continue pressing and squeezing until the entire sheet has been covered and the sponge removes little, or no more, water.

Step 8. Carefully, starting at any corner, peel off the top window screen. Lay down three folded paper towels on top of

each other. When folded, the towels must be wider than the new sheet. If not, get bigger towels, or don't fold them. Pick up the screen with the new sheet on it, and turn it over onto the towels so the new sheet is on the top towel.

Step 9. Apply the sponge as in step 7, this time pushing down with as much force as possible. Apply pressure over the

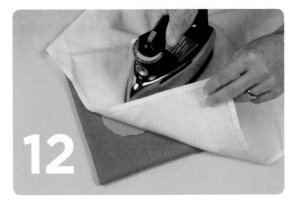

entire new sheet. This is so the new sheet will stay with the towels when the screen is peeled off. Starting slowly at a corner, peel off the window screen, leaving the new sheet on the towels. If the sheet rises with the screen, apply the sponge again with all the force you can. If the sheet still rises with the screen, carefully peel a corner of the new sheet from the screen and separate them with care. At the end of this step, the new sheet should be on top of the paper towels.

Step 10. Fold 3 more paper towels. Place them on top of the new sheet. Take a flat piece of wood, or other flat item, and press down hard on top of the dry towels.

Step 11. Remove the top wet towels and replace them with dry ones. Repeat pressing, replacing wet towels with dry ones

until little water is removed with the dry towels. When the new sheet has become strong enough, lift if off the wet towels beneath it. Replace the wet towels with dry ones. The idea is to get as much water out of the new sheet as possible. *Note:* Do not throw wet towels away. Lay them out to dry and reuse them in future papermaking.

Step 12. Put the new sheet on an ironing board or other dry, clean surface that will not be harmed by heat. Turn a clothes iron to its top heat setting and iron the new sheet dry. Move the iron slowly but steadily, so all parts of the sheet dry at about the same rate. *Note:* Placing a thin cloth over the sheet for ironing is wise. It protects the iron's surface from possible heat-sticky additives that might have been in the recycled paper.

When the sheet is dry, you can shout, wave your arms, sing the national anthem, call neighbors over, and e-mail reporters and photographers from local newspaper, radio, and TV stations. You are an artist and an environmentalist!

Drying and the Teflon Iron

This book advocates placing a thin cloth between the wet paper sheet and the iron. You can try drying sheets by placing a hot iron directly onto the wet sheet, but it's risky. Fiber(s) might stick to the iron, and in two more strokes, the sheet surface can be seriously disrupted. If you don't use a cloth, add to the sheet's safety by using a Teflon-coated iron. Of course, even Teflon can't protect against materials melting in the sheet, especially if you've added bits of plastic or other sensitive elements.

Preparing Pulp

Before I get into more advanced methods, let's talk about pulp. In chapter 2, I talked about where to find pulp and generally how to use it. Now it's time for a few more specifics. For instance, how do you know how much recycled paper and water to put in the blender?

The answer comes from a basic rationale. Fibers are hydrophilic. In water, they swell like a sponge, requiring more room than when dry. There must be enough water to provide room for fiber swelling and fiber movement away from each other. Enough water must be put in the blender to provide that kind of room (*see* Recycling Formulas for Pulp, *at right*). The more new pulp or wastepaper put in, the more water is required. One advantage to the pour method is that you can be more precise about the amount of pulp to use, knowing that *all* of what you prepare will go into the sheet you are making. With the dip method, it's more difficult to know just how much pulp you are capturing in the mold.

Recycling Formulas for Pulp

Pour Molds

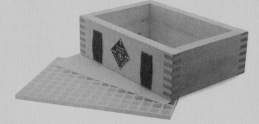

○ For a 5½" × 8½" mold, recycle ¾ of an 8½" × 11" paper sheet with 2 to 2½ cups water.

○ For an 8½" × 11" mold, recycle 1¼ to 1½ sheets of 8½" × 11" paper in 3 to 3½ cups water.

○ For other sizes, follow the general rule of tearing up a piece of paper that is a bit larger than the measurements of the pour mold's deckle. Smaller pieces of paper that together equal sizes listed above can be torn up instead of single pieces.

Dip Molds

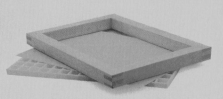

Pulp preparation aims at a pulp thickness in the vat, not at a size of sheet to be made. For a pulp consistency that will make sheets about as thick as stationery, business letters, or book pages, use the following formula.

○ Tear up an 8½" × 11" sheet and add 4 cups water. Run the blender. Pour the recycled pulp into a vat. Repeat until there are 4" or more of pulp in the vat.

○ Dip 2 or 3 sheets and then add pulp to the vat according to the following ratio: Add 3 cups water for every 8½" × 11" sheet. Run the blender. Add the pulp to the vat.

Using New Pulp

For new pulp, follow the directions provided with the pulp. If no directions are provided, experiment. Estimate the amount of pulp needed. Add plenty of water, run the blender, and form a sheet. Here are some pointers:

For a pour mold: If the sheet is too thick, take part of the pulp off the screen. Lower the mold in the water again. Disperse the remaining pulp in the deckle and form a new sheet. Repeat the removal or addition of pulp process until you have the right thickness. The amount of pulp removed or added will indicate how much dry pulp is the right starting amount.

For a dip mold: If the formed sheet is too thick, either add water to the vat or remove pulp with a strainer. Dip a new sheet. Continue this process until the vat's pulp consistency is right.

Thick and Thin Sheets

The sheet thickness can be controlled by varying the ratio of fiber to water in the pulp slurry. With pour molds, thickness can be controlled easily and precisely. With dip molds, it's a bit tricky.

For a pour mold: When recycling, the following provides precise control. Tear and blend a piece of paper that is the same length and width as the deckle. The new sheet made from that pulp will be of the same thickness as the paper recycled. This provides a reference point. To make a new sheet twice as thick, recycle twice the paper, adjusting the amount of water added in the blender. For a sheet half as thick, recycle half as much paper.

When starting with new pulp, preciseness is not as easy. As stated previously, you can guess at how much dry pulp to blend, see what thickness results, and work from that as a reference point. Or, with an appropriate scale, you can weigh out an estimated amount of dry pulp, disperse it in a blender, see what thickness results from that amount, and work mathematically from that as a reference point.

For a dip mold: With dip molds, you must alter the thickness of the slurry in the vat to change the thickness of paper.

Adding pulp will make the next sheets thicker. Adding water or removing pulp with a strainer will make the next sheets thinner.

The thickness fact to remember with the dip mold is that each time you make a sheet of paper, you remove pulp from the vat. The fiber stays out, but the water runs back in. Therefore, the slurry in the vat is thinner, and the following sheet will be thinner, unless you replace the amount of fiber taken out.

Turbulence for Sheet Uniformity

Turbulence in the deckle of a pour hand mold is important to the uniformity of the final sheet. Wiggle your fingers in the slurry or stir with a spoon to disperse the pulp evenly. Don't be shy. It also helps to keep a pour mold low in the vat's water. For dip molds, agitate the pulp before each dip.

Building a Pour Hand Mold

A pour hand mold can be built to any size desired. The dimensions suggested here will produce a hand mold for handmade sheets approximately 5½″ × 8½″.

The pour mold that I designed (shown at right) uses a plastic grid (egg crate) for the support screen instead of a wooden frame topped with hardware cloth. A papermaking screen is placed between the deckle (top frame) and the support screen.

Materials

- Two pieces of finished wood, 1″ × 3″ × 10″ **Ⓐ**
- Two pieces of finished wood, 1″ × 3″ × 5½″ **Ⓑ**
- 1¼″ finishing nails and a hammer (or a pneumatic stapler, if available) **Ⓒ**
- Heavy-duty staples and a staple gun **Ⓓ**
- Two pieces of finished wood, 1″ × 1″ × 10″ **Ⓔ**
- Two pieces of finished wood, 1″ × 1″ × 5½″ **Ⓕ**
- Hardware cloth 5½″ × 10″ **Ⓖ**
- One screen, 5½″ × 10″ (commercial papermaking screen or nonmetal window screen) **Ⓗ**
- Approximately 1 yard of nonadhesive Velcro, 1″ wide **Ⓘ**

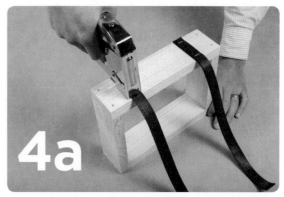

The finished, assembled mold includes the deckle (top frame with straps), the support screen (frame with screen at the bottom), and a papermaking screen (sandwiched between the two).

Instructions

1. Form the deckle by nailing the 1″ × 3″ × 10″ wood pieces to the 1″ × 3″ × 5½″ pieces as shown, to create a rectangular frame.

2. Form the screen support (or mold) by nailing the 1″ × 1″ × 10″ wood pieces to the 1″ × 1″ × 5½″ pieces as shown, to create a rectangular frame. Cover the frame with hardware cloth, and secure it with staples (using either a hammer or staple gun).

3. Place the papermaking screen on top of the screen support and then place the deckle on top of the screen.

4. You'll need to secure the screen support tightly against the deckle for sheet formation, but be able to loosen it to remove the screen support and new sheet after sheet formation. The most efficient way to do this is to add Velcro straps:

o With the support screen in place, measure down the side of the deckle, around the bottom, and up the other side. Cut two strips of the *loop* side of the Velcro to this length.

o Staple one end of each strap to one side of the deckle as shown, about 2″ from either edge.

o On the opposite side of the deckle, place two 2¼″ strips of the *hook* side of the Velcro in the same locations.

o Wrap the looped strip around the deckle, papermaking screen, and support screen, and press the ends onto the 2¼″ hook strips.

Making Paper with a Pour Mold

The basic steps for making paper are essentially the same no matter what technique you use. Since I am recommending the pour method as the easiest to use, the directions are shown using the style of pour hand mold I developed (*see page 50*).

Materials

In addition to the hand mold, you will need a cover screen: a piece of nonmetallic window screen a bit bigger than the sheet you're making. You will also need the supplies listed below (explained in more detail on page 25). If you are using a dip mold, see page 41 for more information.

- Blender
- Vat
- Drain pan
- Sponge
- Couch sheets
- Press bar
- Iron

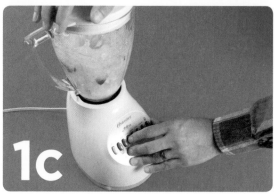

Step 1. Gather your supplies and prepare the pulp (*see page 48*).

Step 2. To assemble the hand mold, place the deckle upside down on a flat surface. Lay the papermaking screen on the deckle, then the screen support. Pull the

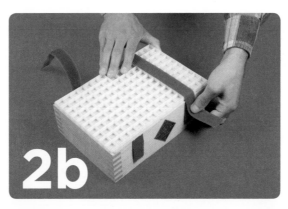

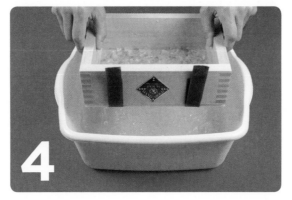

Velcro straps tightly around the grid and press them against the Velcro strips on the opposite side.

Step 3. Turn the hand mold right side up and lower it at a slanted angle into the water in a vat (tub or dishpan). The water must be deep enough to fill the deckle about halfway. Pour pulp into the deckle. By wiggling your fingers or stirring with a plastic spoon, spread the pulp evenly in the water within the deckle.

Step 4. Lift the hand mold out of the water. Hold it level and let all the water drain.

(CONTINUED)

Insider's Tip

The "papermaker's shake" was once part of a journeyman hand-papermaker's skill. **It was vital for certain qualities and characteristics of professional sheets. In general, it entailed shaking the hand mold forward and backward and from side-to-side after it had been lifted from the vat and while the pulp drained. The shake can be done with either pour or dip molds.**

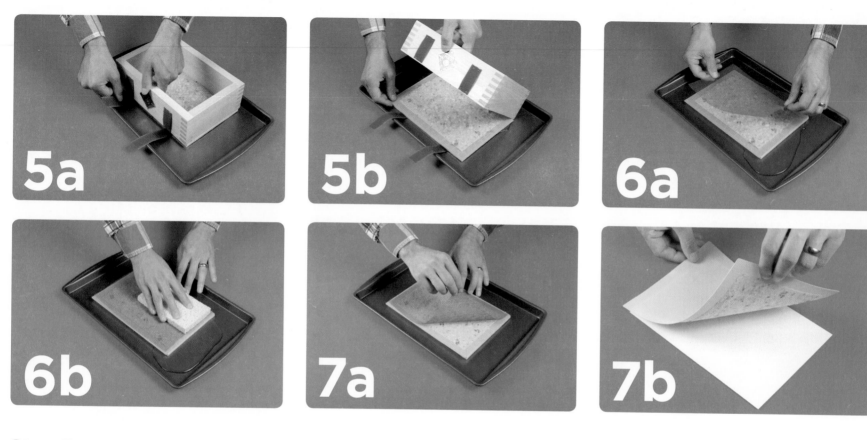

Step 5. Set the hand mold down in a drain pan. Loosen the straps. Lift the deckle up and off of the screen and screen support. If the screen lifts with the deckle, separate the two with your fingernail or a knife blade.

Step 6. Set the deckle aside and carefully put the cover screen over the new sheet resting on the screen support. Press a sponge firmly down on the cover screen. Wring the sponge. Press again. Continue until the sponge removes no more water.

Step 7. Lift a corner of the cover screen carefully and peel it off slowly. If the sheet comes up with the screen, try the other corners. Once the screen is removed, pick up the papermaking screen with the new sheet on it. Turn the screen over, placing the new sheet on a couch sheet. The new sheet will be between the screen and couch sheet.

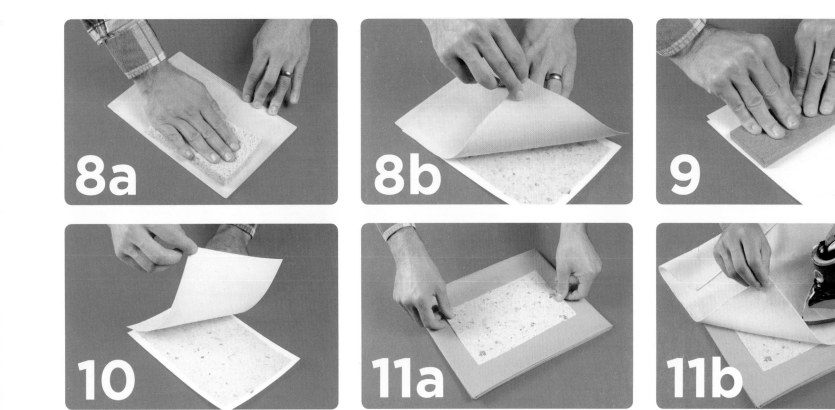

Step 8. Press a sponge firmly all over the screen's surface. Wring the sponge and press again. Repeat until the sponge removes hardly any water. To remove the screen, place one hand on the middle and the other hand at a corner. Slowly lift the corner and peel off the screen, sliding one hand back as the other lifts. If the sheet comes up with the screen, press down hard on each corner and try lifting at each.

Step 9. Put a dry couch sheet over the new sheet. With a press bar, press down hard over the entire surface of the couch sheet until the couch sheet has absorbed as much water as it can.

Step 10. Take off the top couch sheet and then carefully lift one corner of the new sheet. If the sheet is too weak to lift up, repeat step 9 with a dry couch sheet. When

a corner can be lifted, you'll be able to peel it off the couch sheet.

Step 11. Place the new sheet on an ironing board or on a cloth-covered flat surface. Place a thin cloth over the sheet and iron the sheet dry with an iron turned up to maximum heat (no steam).

Drying Options

Heat drying delivers paper immediately, but generally causes the paper to curl and cockle. Drying without heat is better for some paper qualities and delivers a better-looking sheet. For best quality, dry your paper slowly, under pressure. Curing occurs, as well as drying, during time under pressure. The longer the paper is under pressure, the more some qualities will be enhanced. Here's what you do:

Instead of stacking weights on top of the boards, you can use two strong clamps to keep the paper under pressure.

○ Complete step 10 (*see page 55*) and place the paper between two dry couch sheets.

○ Use a press if you have one (*see* Building a Paper Press, *page 34*), or place the sheet (between couch sheets) between two boards and stack weight (for instance, books or cement blocks) on the top board.

○ Wait 20 minutes and exchange the wet couch sheets for dry ones.

○ Wait 2 hours and change couch sheets again. Leave the paper under pressure for 5 or 6 hours more, or better yet, overnight.

○ Check paper for dryness. If it's not too thick, the paper should be dry. If not dry, keep exchanging couch sheets until it is.

Frequently Asked Questions

Q: Can I make paper out of lint from my dryer?

A: Ah, my favorite question not to answer! Paper is cellulose fibers naturally bonded. If your lint is synthetic, the fibers won't bond. They might hang together by friction due to their length. Even if enough of the lint fibers are natural, wet lint is horribly hard to disperse in the vat or in the deckle of a hand mold to form a new sheet. But with a high enough percentage of cellulose fiber and patience to get reasonable dispersion, a hint of lint can impart character to a sheet.

Q: I left pulp in water for a couple of days and it got smelly. Can I still use it?

A: Normally, wet pulp will not become smelly in a day, but it can spoil and smell if left for a couple days in warm weather. When pulp that smells is made into new dry sheets, the paper will normally *not* smell.

Q: What should I do with leftover pulp?

A: You can drain the pulp and store it in an airtight container in your refrigerator. When you're ready to use it, add water and reprocess in a blender. Another option is to drain the pulp and pack it into a *casting* mold. Let it dry, and you will have a paper casting (*see chapter 7*). Never dump leftover pulp down sink drains, as it may cause plumbing problems.

Q: Does using an iron to dry paper hurt the paper?

A: Subtly, yes, but sometimes we are willing to accept the subtle harm to have our paper immediately. Visible harm occurs if you iron in a manner that chars surface fibers, such as leaving the iron too long in one spot or making thick paper that requires too much heat to dry. If it bothers you to iron right on the sheet, you can use a thin cloth over the fibers before applying the iron.

Q: How can I make a "pure" sheet of paper that isn't drab or speckled from ink?

A: Select sections of paper to recycle that have no printing on them. Unprinted margins are the main place to look, but other significant sources of unprinted paper are available. Envelopes and colorful retail store bags deliver large areas of unprinted surface, with subtle to spectacular colors.

Q: I'm getting a thin spot in my paper. What can I do?

A: This usually occurs with professional papermaking screens, which are very finely woven. Consequently, fibers can get stuck easily in the tiny openings. Stuck fibers will cause more to get stuck. Soon a sizeable spot in your screen is plugged. This prevents water from going through those openings. Where water doesn't go, fibers don't go, resulting in a thin spot, or even a hole, in your sheet.

To avoid this problem, rinse your screen in clear water *after every sheet*. Watch your screen for "plugs" and loosen them with water pressure from your sink spray. Apply a stiff brush as the water is running. Dishwasher detergent might help.

Another measure might help: When a thin spot appears in a newly formed sheet, remove pulp in that area of the screen. Scratch the screen surface with a thumbnail or wire brush. Refloat the pulp and form the sheet again. Often, the thin spot does not reoccur.

Q: The papermaking screen is leaving a pattern on my paper. Is there a way to avoid it?

A: Anything touching the wet surface of a newly formed sheet will leave its impression. This is very noticeable with papermaking or cover screens that are as coarse as window screen. If you don't like this effect, try using a thin cloth for a cover screen instead of window screen. I use cut-up cotton bed sheets, but handkerchiefs, cotton dish towels, or lightweight interfacing from the fabric store also work. The cloth's surface (texture, weave, pattern) will be placed on that one side of the sheet. You can also try removing the window screen as soon as possible and after removing as little water as possible. Place a cloth on that surface as well, and keep it on throughout pressing and drying. If enough water remained in the sheet, this procedure may entirely remove the window screen marks. If drying with heat (by ironing), make sure that the cloth can take the heat. This means no synthetics.

Q: I burned out two blenders this year. Is that normal?

A: You are almost surely putting too much paper in the blender and not enough water. When the mixture in the blender is too thick, the motor can't get the blender blades through it. Put in less paper and more water so the blender starts up and runs easily.

A good rule of thumb is not to exceed the equivalent of an 8½" × 11" sheet of copy paper in the blender. Use 3 to 4 cups of water. Adjust measurements when recycling thicker paper. Loaded properly, blenders can last for years.

How to Make Big Sheets

What if you want to make a sheet larger than a standard mold-and-deckle size? It will take a bit of patience, but it can be done. Here's one way to go about it, and you might think up others!

1. Find a smooth hard surface larger than the sheet you are planning. The surface might be a waterproof tabletop, acrylic or laminate sheets, a repurposed window or patio glass door (think safety), or any similar surface you can imagine.

2. Spray it with a release agent (*see page 128*). Form a sheet with your hand mold. Remove the screen and sheet. Turn them upside down and deposit the wet sheet on the hard surface. The screen will be on top. Press a sponge on the screen to remove some, but not all, water. This will "couch" the sheet off the screen onto the surface.

3. Remove the screen. Make a second sheet and couch it onto the hard surface the same way as the first, but slightly overlap the edges of the first and second sheets. Because water is present, the sheets will bond where they are overlapped.

4. Continue this process with as many sheets as necessary to reach the desired sheet size. To smooth overlaps, spray a bit of water on them (not much, just a bit). Tap the overlapped areas with a toothbrush. Mobility of fibers due to being wetted and the action of toothbrush bristles will tend to resurface the sheet where tapped.

5. Put some window screen over the sheet, a section at a time or the entire surface at once, and remove water with a sponge. Press by putting couch sheets or toweling over the sheet and pressing with a large board all at once, or a section at a time with a smaller press board.

6. Press again, as in step 5, using as much pressure as possible. If you have pressed reasonably hard, the sheet can be left on the surface to air dry.

Usually, but not always, the sheet will retain contact with the surface until dry, providing a beautiful evenly dried sheet. Sometimes, contact is too firm and getting the sheet to release is difficult; sometimes, contact will not last and the sheet will release and dry unevenly, creating cockle and curl. In the latter case, use a spray mister to evenly dampen the sheet and press between two boards for several hours.

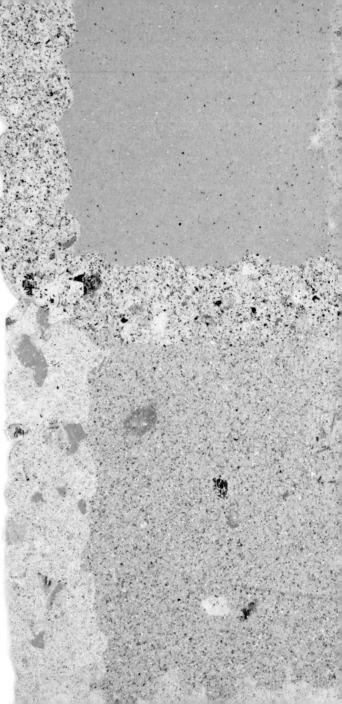

Deckle Variations

Placed on top of the papermaking screen, a deckle determines the shape and size of the sheet. Usually this shape matches the outer size and shape of the mold beneath it. If a piece of flat material with an image cut out of it is placed on top of the screen but under the deckle, the sheet formed will be the size and shape of the cut-out area. You can buy ready-made templates from papermaking suppliers, or make your own from food board, foam core, wood, plastic, or even metal (*see* Handmade Molds and Templates, *pages 80–81*).

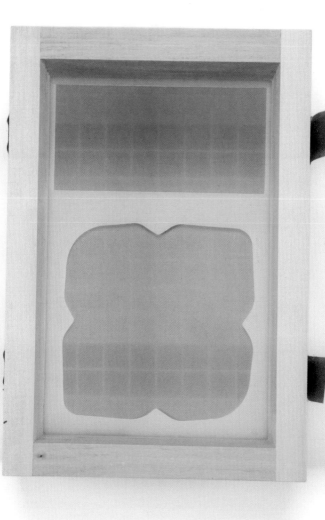

Each paper sheet made with this template produces a folded card and envelope to fit. The plastic version is available online, or trace the template on page 201 onto foam board and cut your own.

Chapter 4
Recycling Techniques

No matter which papermaking process you use, artistic and decorative methods can take you far beyond plain white or colored sheets.

With the techniques in this chapter, you will explore many materials, styles, and moods. Experiment with different options and let your imagination run free. When you find one that strikes your fancy, go with it!

Mottled or Chunky Surface

Run long enough, a blender full of pulp will reduce paper to individual fibers. When the blender is turned off before all the paper comes apart, though, there can be many small paper "chunks" in the resulting pulp. If the paper being recycled is from sheets of several different colors, or of a single sheet on which there were many different ink colors, the chunks could be multicolored.

When a sheet is formed with this kind of pulp, the many individual fibers sink to the screen while the colored chunks tend to float to the surface. This can result in surfaces that are very interesting and pretty. So, by simply experimenting with when to turn off the blender and with what paper or papers to recycle, hundreds of different decorative and artistic sheets can be made.

Step 1. Get paper napkins of three or four different colors.

Step 2. Tear up enough napkins to make a single new sheet (enough to cover an area about 7" square).

Step 3. Put the torn-up napkin pieces into water in a blender.

Step 4. Run the blender only 4 seconds.

Step 5. Make a sheet of paper, using whatever technique you prefer (*see chapter 3*).

Variations

For different batches, try some of the following options:

○ **Run the blender for different lengths of time.**

○ **Recycle single sheets on which there are many different colors of ink.**

○ **Recycle pieces of two or more papers of different colors at the same time.**

○ **Tear up the paper into smaller or larger pieces, or into both small and large pieces.**

○ **Recycle a sheet printed with words. Turn the blender off early. See whether single letters and/or whole words appear on the surface of your new sheet.**

Writing on Mottled Surfaces

The mottled surface technique can make impressive handmade papers and greeting cards, but they can be difficult, or impossible, to write on. The writing gets lost in the mottling. To fix this problem, use a turkey baster to lay a smaller, even layer of solid white or colored pulp on a second screen and then pulp layer (*see page 78*) it onto the mottled surface. This provides a writing patch. It can be made in different shapes.

(*see page 78*)

Frequently Asked Questions

Q: How do I put seeds in paper? Will they grow?

A: Seeds can be added to pulp for papermaking. Add them after blending the pulp and before forming sheets. (See the project on page 194.) Large, flat seeds are easiest to embed. Whether planted paper will bloom and grow depends on many factors, including seed quality, paper thickness, and planting conditions, but brief exposure to water during paper making will not cause germination.

A seed consultant suggests that most hardy seeds are good candidates for making plantable paper. He recommends cosmos, marigold, calendula, poppies, and cornflower seeds. In his opinion, it is safe to iron dry sheets with these embedded seeds. Seed paper covered with a thin layer of dirt, plus warmth, water, and sunshine will, hopefully, bring on sprouts.

Surface Embedment

Anything that is thin, flat, and flexible can be locked onto the surface of a sheet of handmade paper by the top layers of fibers. Even the thinnest sheet of paper is made up of numerous layers of small papermaking fibers. Suitable materials can be put down into the last of the water as the fibers descend toward the papermaking screen. The final fibers will attach the material into the sheet's surface. A few experiments will show you what works and what doesn't.

For this technique, you want the pulp to drain slowly, to allow time for the added elements to embed. For best results, recycle paper that results in a slower draining pulp, or add more water. The deeper the water in the hand mold, the longer it will take to drain. Also, use a bit more pulp, because surface embedment works better on a somewhat thicker sheet (think greeting card thickness).

An embedded strip of burlap creates a stream connecting two lakes, or maybe just adds a burst of texture.

Step 1. Prepare pulp by running paper in a blender. Run the blender until few or no chunks of paper are left.

Step 2. Select something to embed. This could be leaves or other bits of nature, ribbon, fabric scraps, or your favorite character cut from the Sunday comics. Dip the item into one of the containers of pulp. This will make it wet and possibly deposit some papermaking fibers on its edges. Set it nearby in some manner that it can be quickly and easily picked up.

Step 3. Start the papermaking process by pouring pulp into the mold. Immediately grab the cutout. As the last water and fibers descend toward the screen, firmly push the cutout below the surface of the still-draining water and onto the fibers already lying on the screen. The remaining fibers should descend and tie the embedded item into the sheet's surface.

Step 4. Continue the papermaking process as usual (*see chapter 3*).

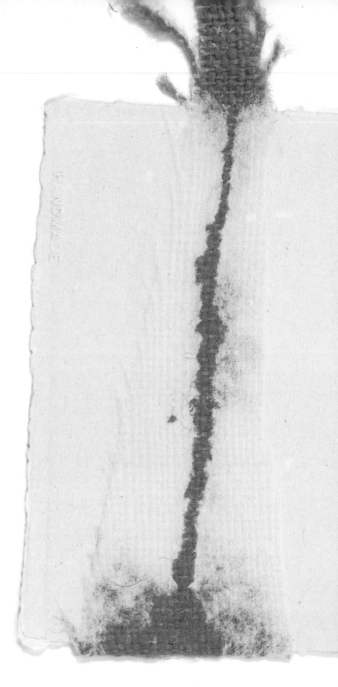

Napkinization

If you can pronounce it, you can do it! Anyone can transform an art napkin into a beautiful art card or sheet. Here's how it's done.

1. Cut an interesting art image from a napkin. Peel the image to a single-ply piece. (This can be a little tricky, but it's definitely do-able.)

2. Put the rest of the napkin into your blender and recycle it into pulp. Add other fiber if you wish, but it's not necessary; the resulting sheet will be stronger than the typical napkin. Form a sheet. Take the wet sheet from the mold.

3. Pick up the cutout by hand or with tweezers and carefully place it where you want it on the surface of the wet sheet. (If the paper is to become a card, place it on the right-hand side to allow for a center fold.) This takes care and maybe a little practice. If you can hold onto the cutout at opposite ends and drop the center down first, you can let the rest of the cutout roll down onto the surface.

4. When the cutout is down, you will see the water rapidly absorb it into the sheet's surface. Subsequently press and dry the sheet as usual (*see pages 54–55*).

Using Botanicals

You can achieve some truly beautiful results by adding selections from nature into your papermaking. Let fall leaves fall into your handmade paper projects! The paper will be unique; no other card or sheet will ever have that leaf. If the leaf is from one of your trees, it has within it whatever work, effort, and time you have put into the tree's care, or simply your appreciation for the tree beauty. The paper you make can be used for all types of projects from home décor to greeting cards.

If the paper is dried under pressure, leaves can be taken from your lawn directly to your papermaking area and used without any preparation. I also like the effect of placing leaves between pages of big books for a week or so; most leaves respond beautifully to this or any other extended pressing. This method also works for embedding flower petals onto your paper. Here are some tips that have proven successful. Add them to your own good ideas.

Leaves and garden foliage are as striking in handmade paper as they were in lawn and garden.

○ Cut stems or flower heads as soon after blooming as possible. The more petals are exposed to the sun, the less pigment they'll retain in handmade paper.

○ The best time to harvest flowers is in the morning after dew disappears.

○ Press leaves and petals in an old phone book or flower press to embed flat. To save whole flower heads, hang stems in bunches upside down in a dry, cool place, or on a rack where air can circulate.

○ To save an entire vase bouquet: After prime blooming is past, do not replenish water. Let the bouquet dry right in the vase. This can take weeks to months, depending on local climate.

○ When flowers are completely dry, store pressed flowers on labeled pages in sheet protectors in a binder. Store dried flower heads in labeled brown paper bags.

○ Record the flower name (if you know it!), where you found it, and what month it bloomed (for instance, mid-July). Then, if you find something you really like, you can look for it again next year.

Frequently Asked Questions

Q: What are the best flowers to use for papermaking?

A: Actually, any flowers can be used, but some petals bleed color. Roses are an example. Many flowers fade over time. Consider parts that are sufficiently small or formed in such a way that they can be successfully embedded. Ferns are quite dependable. Flowers likely to retain color are coral bells, pink and blue larkspur, bachelor buttons, red or purple bee balm (monarda), marigolds, sunflowers, angel wings (from potpourri), and most any color of statice.

Botanical Difficulties

Botanicals frequently float to the top and thus evade becoming tied down to the sheet's surface. While pulp is draining, carefully push the botanical beneath the surface of undrained pulp. Be careful not to push so hard that fibers already on the screen are disturbed, which could seriously or fatally flaw the sheet.

Some botanicals leach out plant elements during sheet drying, creating a corona of stainlike color in the dried sheet. This can be attractive or unattractive. It sometimes seems the less time the botanical is wet, the less the corona. For such foliage, drying with an iron would be best. With some foliage, soaking ahead of time seems to help. Some foliage seems to leach hardly at all. Consequently, it's difficult to generalize. Making test sheets can be helpful. Dry one sheet slowly under pressure and a second sheet with an iron. Soak some of the same foliage in advance to see whether presoaking helps. Again, personal experience and observation are your best teachers. May nature be kind to all of us.

The Tissue Issue

Let's admit it, tissue as an "in use" product just isn't all that glamorous. It doesn't appear in majestic frames hanging on the walls of upscale classic art museums. All in all, it's just sort of a ho-hum item, like "Pass me a tissue, I've got to sneeze." But, in hand papermaking, tissue paper is an exciting way to add bright colors. I thought I had exhausted the possibilities with napkins, but working with tissue has really set my creative juices buzzing. Use tissue in the same way as for napkinization (*see page 65*), and let the fun begin!

Earth Day Project: Street Sheet

The point of Earth Day is to do good to, and for, the environment. One part of this is to limit stuffing junk into the Earth through landfills. As a symbol of limiting landfills, and to honor your Earth, make a "street sheet."

A street sheet gathers up odds and ends that would normally be discarded and keeps them out of the Earth by putting them into a sheet of paper. What might be found in a street sheet? Some of mine show ribbons, gum/candy wrappers, threads, window screen bits, grass clippings, flower stems, and what looks like an old shoestring.

Making a street sheet is just like embedding botanicals in paper (*see page 66*), but instead of adding botanicals to pulp in the deckle or vat, you add street items. This year, observe Earth Day by making a street sheet, or at least recycle some landfill-bound paper into a beautiful new handmade sheet.

On Earth Day, what you find on the street goes into your sheet.

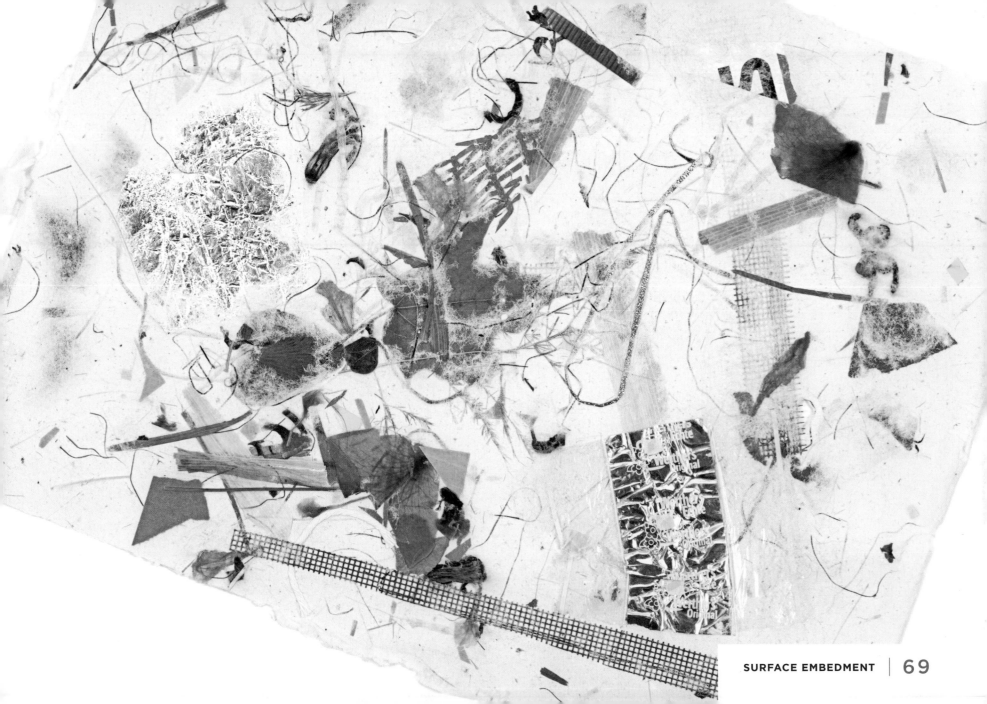

Internal Embedment

A sheet of paper is made up of little individual fibers. A variety of things can be mixed with the fibers and made a part of the sheet. These nonfiber additions, like colorful threads, can make the sheet beautiful and distinctive. But do not add too much nonfiber material, or the papermaking fiber's ability to keep the sheet together will be destroyed.

Materials can be added to the fibers in the blender when paper is being recycled into pulp. If you want to maintain the shape of something, such as leaves, keep them out of the blender or they will shred into small bits and pieces. It's best not to add string or threads in the blender. They tend to wrap around the blender blades. Experience will show the best time to add specific materials.

When you make this sheet, add materials for embedment *after* the source paper has been run in a blender.

Step 1. Run paper in a blender to make pulp.

Step 2. Pour the pulp into containers and add many short and longer pieces of different-colored threads to each container. (Threads show up nicely; fabric will work as long as the pieces aren't too big or thick.) Stir the threads into the pulp.

Step 3. Form a new sheet of paper using your papermaking method of choice (*see chapter 3*). With the pour method, as you pour the pulp into the mold, threads and other materials tend to migrate toward the sides. Watch for this and use something like a plastic kitchen scraper to move the threads into the body of the paper.

More Experiments

For different batches, try some of the following options:

O Place one or two dried leaves of trees or flowers into the blender with the paper to be recycled. If you have tree leaves, use the stems also. Green leaves can be used, but often this results in a greenish tinge around the foliage pieces in the final sheet. But you might like that effect!

O To combine threads, ribbon lengths, leaves, and grass in a sheet, first put leaves and grass into the blender with paper to be recycled. Then add the threads and ribbons to the pulp when it is in containers just before pouring. Ribbon and thread tend to float; they might need to be pushed down below the surface of the draining water in order to be made secure in the new sheet.

O Try glitter. Add it either in the blender and/or in the containers just before pouring (for more about glitter, *see page 76*).

The Confetti Sheet

There is something about the word "confetti" that excites the mind. Can you put confetti, with all of its innate fun-and-frolic connotation, on the surface of your handmade paper? Yes, but keep in mind a prime personality trait of confetti; bits tend to fly away when the dried sheet is handled. In most instances, though, this tendency is not so serious as to cause one to totally ignore all the fun a confetti sheet can provide.

So give it a try. Add the confetti bits to the pulp after blending. For best results, rock the hand mold as the pulp is draining to encourage the pulp to wash over the confetti bits and hold them to the paper.

Chapter 5
Pulp Magic

SWIRL

FRESH

Once you've mastered the basics of papermaking, then the fun really begins! This chapter covers a variety of ways you can work with pulp, including ways to add color and glitter, and how to layer it and paint with it. As you practice these techniques, you will walk through the worldwide wonderland of waste paper!

You will find amazing colors — pastels and hues of a thousand shades residing in dyed fibers. On these papers, you will find expensive and exotic inks. The entire world of waste paper is as mixable as the colors on an artist's palette. You can find gleam and glisten in paper/foil combinations and in the heavy metallic inks that shatter into a thousand points of light in the blender. Take the walk.

Getting Color: Dyeing vs. Recycling

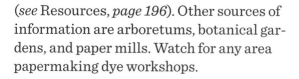

People often ask me how to dye paper, and my initial reaction is, "If you want to make decorative and artistic papers, why spend your time on dyeing?" All the colors, hues, and pastels of dyed fibers you can ever imagine are in your wastebasket, for free. And remember: Wastepaper does not mean waste fiber. These fibers have been professionally dyed with high technology and expert supervision at pulp or paper mills. You are not likely to match their quality at home for some time, if ever.

Also, color for handmade paper is readily available by recycling papers printed with colored ink. Take time to notice subdued or brilliant inks on papers. Then put those colors to use by adding them to your handmade papers.

However, if you want to try your hand at dyeing, or if you absolutely must have what some natural dye offers, just keep in mind that the in depth world of dyeing is complex, made up of pots, pans, multi-hour soaks, hot and cold water, acidity and alkalinity, plant and berry squishing and squashing, straining, lots of time, some expense, and more.

If all of this interests you, check other papermaking books for specific recipes (*see* Resources, *page 196*). Other sources of information are arboretums, botanical gardens, and paper mills. Watch for any area papermaking dye workshops.

Glitter and Glisten

Many people respond to glitter in paper. Soft or brilliant reflections from a paper surface, as it is turned at different angles to the light, can surprise, please, and delight. You don't need to buy glitter, although you can if you like. Glittery effects can be achieved by using a number of recycled materials. Simply stated, foil is where you find it, attached to or separate from paper. If you see it, try it.

A problem can arise when using foils: The shiny bits can be pounded into small, dense wads by the blender. Sometimes, this doesn't matter, especially if drying is done without heat and under considerable pressure. When foil wads do become a problem, it can help to reduce the amount of time the foil part of the paper is in the blender. Total flatness of foil pieces can best be achieved by cutting the foil to desired sizes with scissors and adding them to the pulp in the deckle, after the pulp has been blended (*see* Surface Embedment, *page 64*).

Glitter also comes in near-powder form in bottles, available at your local craft store or online. This small-size flake or near-powder glitter can be added in either the blender or the deckle. The blender affects some types, but not others.

Recycled Glitter Sources

- **Envelopes with gold foil liners**
- **Packaging materials with foil in their makeup**
- **Food wrapping that is totally foil, such as margarine stick wrappers**
- **Gift wrap that is partially foil or laminated to foil**
- **Gum and candy wrappers**
- **Cut-up aluminum foil**
- **Paper and cards with metallic inks**

Frequently Asked Questions

Q: Why doesn't glitter stay in my paper?

A: It is just resting on the surface rather than actually a part of the sheet. In the pulp in the deckle, glitter tends to float. To tie glitter down, there must be fibers over at least part of each glitter particle. Putting glitter in the blender can help, as does vigorously rocking the mold in all directions as the water drains. Try putting very few fibers in the deckle with glitter and literally forming a very thin sheet of fibers and glitter. Then pulp layer (*see page 78*) the thin sheet onto the surface of your regular sheet. Tying glitter securely into a sheet takes attention. Tying down 100 percent of the glitter may never happen.

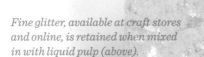

Fine glitter, available at craft stores and online, is retained when mixed in with liquid pulp (above).

Glitter from foil in a recycled envelope stays put in the finished sheet (right).

Pulp Layering

Just as single fibers bond to single fibers in the presence of water, batches of fibers bond to other batches of fiber if enough water is present. This means you can make a sheet, remove no water from it, make a second sheet of a different color, shape, or size, remove no water from it either, and put it down as a layer on the surface of the first sheet. If the two layers are then handled as a single sheet for dewatering, pressing, and drying, the layers will in fact become a single sheet by the end of the process.

There can be as many layers as the papermaker can handle, but water must always be present. Remove no water until all layers are in place. Pulp layering opens broad horizons of art and decorative expression, especially in association with recycling, which provides endless types and colors of pulp, free and instantly.

For this technique, you will make two separate sheets. One will be regular-sized, and the second will be smaller, which requires a second, smaller mold. This can be a small tin can, cookie cutters with high sides, or any number of found items. You also can custom-cut a template (*see* Handmade Molds and Templates, *page 80*). You will be making the second sheet before the first sheet is taken off the papermaking screen, so have an appropriate size square of window screen ready for the second sheet.

Step 1. Make a sheet of paper with your technique of choice, using a single pulp color.

Step 2. Lift the new sheet and the papermaking screen straight up off the support screen and place them down on a surface that will catch any draining water. Do not press any water from the new sheet. Set up a second papermaking screen for the second sheet.

Step 3. Blend pulp of a different color in your blender. Because the second sheet is much smaller, you will need much less pulp.

Step 4. Make the second sheet of paper in the smaller mold (*see* Second Sheet Option, *on the next page*).

Step 5. Begin to "layer" this second new sheet onto the surface of the first new sheet by lifting the papermaking screen and new sheet off the support screen.

Step 6. Hold the second new sheet on its screen in mid-air and turn them over (so the papermaking screen is on top and the new sheet is on the bottom). The new sheet will not fall off unless it is very thick. Lower the smaller new sheet carefully down onto the surface of the first, larger sheet. (You can place the smaller sheet wherever you wish on the larger sheet's surface.)

Step 7. Press a sponge down firmly on the top papermaking screen. Wring water from the sponge and repeat, pressing over the entire surface.

Step 8. Lift the top papermaking screen carefully. The smaller sheet should separate from the papermaking screen and stay bonded to the surface of the larger sheet.

Note: If the smaller sheet tends to rise with the screen, lay the screen back down and apply pressure again with the sponge. Some pulps tend to stick to the papermaking screen. If separation still fails to occur after more pressure has been applied, either try to peel the new sheet off, or simply wash the sheet off the screen and make a new sheet with new pulp from a different type of paper.

Step 9. Continue with the regular papermaking process (*see page 55*) just as though the two-layer sheet were a single sheet.

Second Sheet Option

You might want to set up a second screen for your second pulp layer. Lay a support screen or a piece of fine hardware cloth over a bucket, large bowl, or cookie sheet with sides. This provides an open surface on which to work with one or more mold shapes, allowing plenty of room for a flat template (*see page 80*) or other options. You can use the same arrangement for pulp painting.

Any time you make a separate layer of pulp, remember that the layer will be flipped over and reversed on the paper background. This is especially important when making letters. Plastic letter templates (see Resources) can make the job even easier. These letters are from a Jello-cutting alphabet found in a second-hand store.

Handmade Molds and Templates

Molds. As noted previously, the size and shape of your paper depends on the size and shape of the mold you use — and the possibilities are endless! In addition to tin cans and other recycled containers, you can use cookie cutters and aspic cutters for creative shaping of both papers and pulp layers. To fully customize your own unique shapes, see the instructions on the next page.

Templates. Templates are an efficient way to make paper in a shape you want. A template has the same outer measurement as the deckle, and it slides between the deckle and papermaking screen (*see page 59*). Templates for standard size envelopes are available for purchase, but you can make your own from foam core, wood, or other materials with sufficient rigidity and thickness. My favorite recycled approach is to trace a shape onto food board (the Styrofoam-like material under meats and pastries from the grocery store) and cut it out with a battery-operated hot wire foam cutter, readily available at craft stores. You can use a utility knife instead, but hot wire makes a cleaner cut. See Resources for a few template options.

To make paper with a template, slide the template into place and form a sheet in the usual way. Carefully lift the template off the papermaking screen before the first step of water removal. Nudge any fibers clinging to the template onto the newly formed paper with a finger or toothpick. Press and dry in the usual way.

Custom Brass Form

Sometimes, it's impossible to find just the right cookie cutter shape for an inspired project. You can make your own metal form with brass strips from the hardware store. Brass strips are bendable and corrosion-resistant. And, they're recyclable!

Instructions

1. Draw or trace a shape on a piece of paper.

2. Place the vertical edge of the brass strip along the outline. Work the strips into shape, using your hands where possible. Tight angles and curves require the use of the pliers. *Note:* Do not begin at a corner. Start on a gentle curve or straight area of the design where it is easier to glue strips together. Plan for a 1″ overlap at the ends, or any time you need to attach two strips together to make a larger mold.

3. Mix epoxy and spread it on overlapping ends of the strips. Hold glued section together with a small clamp, as advised by epoxy package directions. If the area is too small to clamp, wrap masking tape around the glued section to secure it. You can continue making bends once the glue has set.

Materials

- Paper and pencil
- Shape template (optional)
- Brass strips: several 12″ long, ½″ wide, 0.016 thickness
- Large needle nose or flat nose pliers
- Epoxy
- Small clamp
- Masking tape

An Option to Brass

You can also cut strips from a disposable aluminum pie tin and shape them as desired. These pie tin strips make good molds because they are very sturdy, but still flexible enough to bend into interesting shapes.

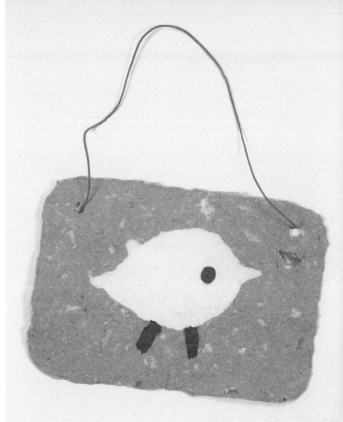

Wall Art

When it comes to pulp layering (*see page 78*), anything goes, from simple to complex. The white bird was made with handmade pie-tin molds and dabs of black pulp. Once the two layers were pressed together and dried, holes were punched on both sides of the top, with yarn added for hanging.

Crafty Tip

You can make these coasters one at a time, as instructed, or use a larger piece of mesh screen and make them side-by-side, two, four, or more at a time.

Coasters

Here's a great introductory project for pulp layering and painting. These coasters have one solid color on the back side or bottom, another solid color on the top, and multicolor rays on top of that. For instance, the color on the bottom of the brown-and-yellow coasters is orange. Endless possibilities!

Materials

- O Pulp in assorted colors, separated into different containers
- O 4"-diameter circle mold (large-sized tin can works well)
- O Papermaking screen
- O Sponge
- O Pulp gun (*see page 27*)
- O Couching sheets
- O Paper towels
- O Boards or books (for weights)
- O 3"- or 4"-diameter circle template (optional)
- O Utility knife (optional)

Instructions

1. Pour the pulp color you want on the bottom into a circle shape. For a nice, thick coaster, pour the pulp generously; it should be approximately ¼" deep in the mold before draining the water.

2. Move the circle and screen to the side to drain. Do not press or iron dry.

3. Pour the pulp color you want on top into a circle shape. Once the pulp has drained a bit, carefully turn the screen upside down and line it up on top of the previous circle. Press lightly on the screen with a sponge to release the top circle.

4. Use the pulp gun and fresh colors to make patterns on the top circle, as desired.

5. Couch the coaster(s) to remove some of the water (*see page 55*) and leave them to dry overnight pressed between paper towels and a couple of boards or books (*see page 56*). They will take considerably longer to dry than usual, due to their thickness.

6. Finish dried coasters by using the circle template and utility knife to trim into clean-edged circles or simply leave them with a natural edge.

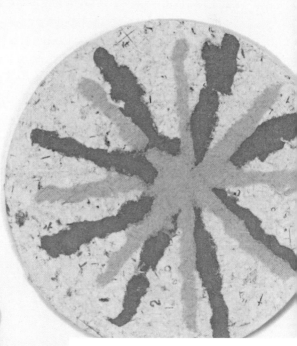

Pulp Painting

It's easy to make a pulp "gun." With it, you can "shoot" pulp onto a screen in a variety of shapes or abstract patterns. You can shoot one color and then reload and shoot another color. With good aim, you can form single or multicolor images, such as numbers, letters, scenes, or abstract patterns. Combined with the pulp layering technique, you can place your numbers, letters, scenes, or patterns on the surface of a regular sheet, making beautiful decorated paper or works of art. Pulp guns can be made with any plastic squeeze bottle that has a lid with a nozzle, such as some containers for mustard and ketchup (*see page 27*).

What follows are two different ways to paint with pulp, either directly on the first wet sheet or indirectly, painting freehand layers on a second screen and transferring them to the first sheet. Experiment with thicker or thinner pulp in the pulp gun.

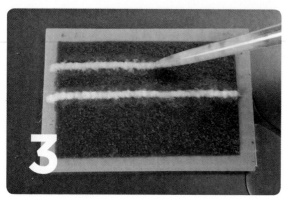

Direct Pulp Painting

Step 1. Set up a papermaking screen on top of a drain rack and place them in a drain pan. Make a background sheet, leaving it as wet as possible on the papermaking screen. If necessary, spray it to rewet.

Step 2. Recycle a different color of paper in the blender, running it until there are no chunks left. Pour the pulp into a plastic squeeze bottle or turkey baster. Fill the bottle half full and put the lid on. Be sure the nozzle is open.

Step 3. Paint directly on the wet background sheet.

Step 4. Press and dry the sheet.

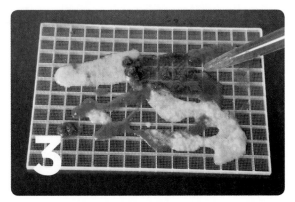

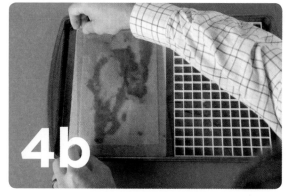

Indirect Pulp Painting

Step 1. Make a sheet and leave it wet on the papermaking screen. Set up a second papermaking screen on a support screen, as with pulp layering (*see page 79*).

Step 2. Recycle a different color of paper in the blender, running it until there are no chunks left. Pour the pulp into a plastic mustard or ketchup squeeze bottle.

Fill the bottle half full and put the lid on. Be sure the nozzle is open. Another option is to mix several different colors in paper cups and dip into them one at a time with a turkey baster.

Step 3. Aim the pulp gun nozzle down at the screen, within 2″ of the surface. Give the pulp gun a short, gentle squeeze and

shoot little patches of pulp onto the screen as desired. Experiment with harder, longer squeezes as well, and feel free to try different colors and thicker or thinner pulp slurries in the pulp gun.

Step 4. Pick up the secondary screen and layer it onto the sheet you made earlier by turning it upside down onto the first sheet. The fibers will bond and transfer. Multiple layers can be painted and transferred as desired. Press and dry the sheet.

More Pulp Painting Experiments

For different batches, try some of the following options:

O Use thick and thinner pulps in the bottle.

O Use different types of plastic bottles with larger or smaller nozzle openings.

O Hold the bottle at different angles to the screen. At the same time, try squeezing harder and softer.

O Try writing with the gun. Squirt pulp out into the form of your initials. Make sure to write the letters backward when doing pulp painting, so they will transfer and read the right way around when placed on another paper sheet.

O Try simple drawings, such as a tree, using two or more colors.

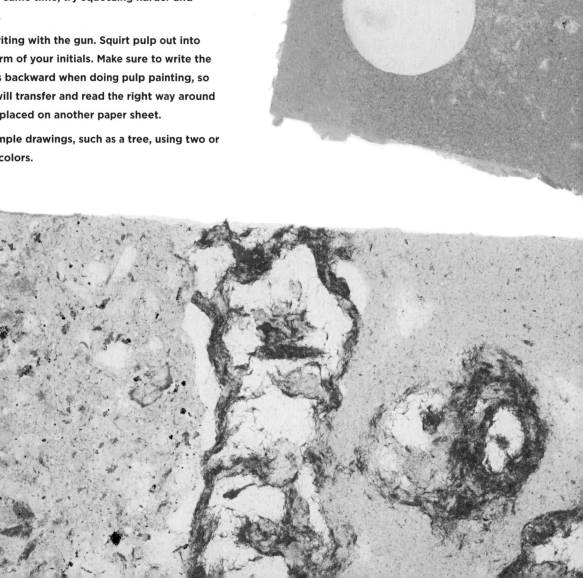

Avoid piling up pulp in high ridges or mounds. **Put down thin little patches, patterns, and lines. Adding water to the pulp in the bottle will help keep pulp from getting too thick on the screen. Once you've gotten a feel for the process, you can experiment with thicker and thinner pulp in the bottle.**

Adding Color in the Deckle

After a sheet's worth of pulp has been poured into the deckle of a pour hand mold, you can throw in many other interesting components. These can include other colored pulps, botanicals, glitter, strips of fabric, and so on. It's a whole world unto itself. Adding color at this point is easy and leads to all kinds of unique results. The following instructions work best for a pour mold that is strapped together, so you have your hands free to apply other colors while the mold rests in the vat.

Step 1. Prepare a sheet's worth of pulp. White is probably the best to show off the colors you want to add. Pour the pulp into a container and put it aside.

Step 2. Prepare several colors of pulp by recycling colored papers in a blender. Put each in a separate cup and set aside.

Step 3. Use the pulp from step 1 to begin making a sheet of paper, but pause with the mold still in the vat.

Step 4. Draw colored pulp into a turkey baster. Using just a bit of gentle pressure on the baster's bulb, shoot some of the colored pulp into the white pulp at a corner of the deckle.

Step 5. Repeat the action with each of the other colored pulps in separate corners of the deckle.

Step 6. Complete by making your paper as usual.

Variations

This technique offers great room for exploration, experimentation, and a wide range of unique and wonderful papers:

O In step 4, try holding the baster at different levels; use different amounts of pressure on the baster bulb; use different thicknesses of colored pulp slurries in the baster; or put the baster end down into the pulp and shoot.

O Try different pulp guns (syrup dispenser, mustard container, and so on). Try anything your imagination can uncover as a way to enter colored pulps into the pulp already in the deckle.

O These sheets will likely be two-sided. Dispersion on one side of the sheet will be different than on the other because the colored pulp tends to sink. Close observation can lead to further manipulation of this phenomenon and how it works.

Frequently Asked Questions

Q: Can I put recycled paper through my home printer?

A: I am not an expert on printers, but I do print often on my handmade paper. My inkjet printer has suffered no discernable ill effects. I do not know about laser or any other type of home printer. Common sense and some experimentation indicate that sheets that are too thick or thin will present problems. The more pressure you apply during drying, the better the final paper will be for printing. Check your owner's manual for more tips.

Color(s) can be added to the pulp in the deckle, gently or with force.

Bordering

Here is another way to add color in the deckle, after the water has drained from the first sheet. Use this technique to put a border on one edge or entirely around a sheet. You can even achieve a self-framing effect by forming a mat that becomes part of the paper sheet.

Direct Bordering

Step 1. Prepare enough pulp for one sheet. Prepare several colors of pulp for adding as the border or frame.

Step 2. Follow the basic papermaking procedure through step 4 (*see page 53*). Once the paper is drained, set the mold down in a drain pan.

Step 3. Draw colored pulp into a pulp gun. Drop and dribble the colored pulp along the edge of the sheet next to the deckle, on one or more edges. Repeat with as many colored pulps as you wish.

Step 4. Loosen the mold straps and continue with papermaking as usual.

Keep the point of the baster near the deckle wall and release pulp very gently.

Indirect Bordering

Step 1. Prepare enough pulp for one sheet. Prepare several colors of pulp for adding as the border or frame.

Step 2. Make a full-sized sheet of paper, following the basic papermaking procedure through step 5 (*see page 54*). Once you've removed the deckle, set the wet sheet in a drain pan.

Step 3. Set up a separate papermaking screen over a drain pan or bucket and set the deckle on top. Draw colored pulp into a pulp gun and dribble the colored pulp onto the window screen, inside the deckle and along the edges. Leave the center of the screen open.

Step 4. Remove the deckle and lift the window screen. Carefully turn it over so the pulp is on the bottom.

Step 5. Match the outside edges of the pulp carefully to the outside edges of the new sheet and lower the edged screen onto the new sheet. Apply a sponge to the window screen to remove water. After removing as much water as possible, carefully lift the window screen. The colored pulps will remain on the edge(s) of the new sheet.

Step 6. Finish making the paper as usual.

Crafty Tip

The amount of pulp you apply as a border or self-frame depends on your taste. Applying pulp sparingly will keep sheet edges more uniformly thick with the sheet's center. If you want more of a distinct frame, more pulp might be in order.

indirect

direct

Chapter 6
More Fun Things to Try

It would be impossible to include every technique for creative papermaking in this book. Truly, there are as many ideas as there are people to think them up!

If you're hooked on papermaking and want to try some new effects, this chapter provides a sampling to whet your appetite even further.

Pin Drawing

When you dip a pin in pulp slurry, it will pick up fibers. You can then use the pin to "draw" with those fibers on the surface of a newly formed wet sheet. By lowering the pin horizontally to the wet sheet and dropping the point onto the surface, the pin fibers and surface fibers will create a bond. When you pull the pin away, the fibers will slide off and be deposited onto the surface in a line. With practice, you can make curved lines, lay down several lines adjacent to each other, and make thicker lines. Pin drawing can be a very sensitive medium for artistic expression.

"Pin drawing" and "patience" both start with a P.

Crafty Tips

O **Bend the pin just below its head to create something to grip. You don't want your fingertips to touch the sheet's surface.**

O **Thick and thin slurries lay down different kinds of lines. See the difference by experimenting with thick, thin, and medium-thick slurries. You also can make lines thicker by laying down several thin lines side-by-side.**

O **Although I work with pins, there is room for discovery in trying thin wires. Bending a thin wire would be easier than bending a pin, and pins tend to break, rather than bend.**

O **The line of fibers can be manipulated on the sheet. You can use the point of the pin to move them a bit to one side or to straighten the line's edges. This is delicate and requires a careful touch. The point of the pin must engage with the added fibers only, or you might tear your sheet.**

O **Use short containers for the pulp you'll be drawing with. Tall containers make it difficult to get the pin down into the pulp. It also helps to tip the container to one side when dipping the pin.**

Step 1. Make a full-sized sheet of paper, following the basic papermaking procedure through step 6 (*see page 54*), but don't put on the cover screen.

Step 2. Prepare a thick slurry of colored pulp. Divide it by pouring into two small containers. Add water to one container to thin out the pulp.

Step 3. Draw a shape on the new sheet's surface by dipping a pin into the thick slurry and lifting out some fibers. Lower the pin horizontally, but with a bit of a slant, so the fibers near the pin point will touch the sheet's surface first. Lower the remaining fibers onto the sheet.

Step 4. Slide the pin slowly out of the pulp. Because the fibers touching the surface will have bonded slightly, the wet fibers on the pin will generally slide off as the pin is withdrawn. By repeated dipping, make the line as long as you wish.

Step 5. Dip the pin into the thinner pulp slurry and experiment with drawing more lines. Note the differences between the lines.

Step 6. Complete your drawing. Put the cover screen over the new sheet and finish making the paper.

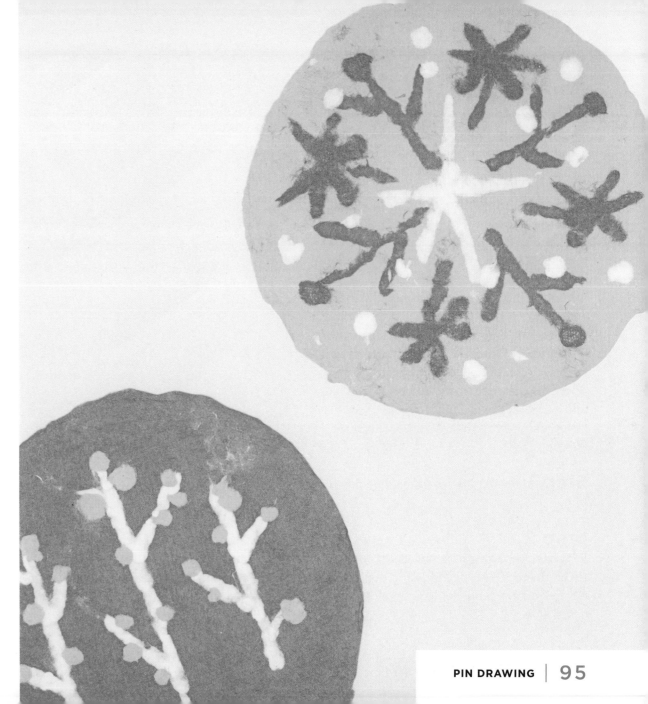

Edge Dipping

If you dip one edge of a pour hand mold into water, you have a pool over that side of the papermaking screen, into which you can pour colored pulps. The width and length of the pool is something you can play with by raising or lowering the hand mold's edge in the water. When you lift the mold from the water, there will be a strip of pulp on one side of the papermaking screen that is straight on one edge and ragged on the other. You can use this as a secondary layer and add it on top of a newly formed wet sheet, using the pulp layering technique (*see page 78*).

Step 1. Prepare three different colors of pulp.

Step 2. Make a full-sized sheet of paper, following the basic papermaking procedure through step 6 (*see page 54*), but don't put on the cover screen. Set this sheet aside to drain a bit.

Step 3. Use a second papermaking screen (the cover screen can be used) in the mold and dip the mold at a slanted angle into the vat. Water will come up over the edge of the papermaking screen. Keep the mold at a steep angle, so deep water covers about one-quarter of the screen.

Step 4. Hold the mold steady. Into the pool of water above the screen, pour different-colored pulps in different places. Don't pour in too much pulp. Add glitter if desired.

Step 5. Lift the mold out of the water. For the first effort, lift it straight up, not changing the angle. In later efforts, try lifting the mold out with a bit of a scooping action. This will cause water and some pulp to wash a little higher on the screen as the mold is lifted. This can result in a ragged, possibly dramatic, edge as the pulp drains on the screen.

Step 6. Use the pulp layering technique (*see page 78*) to transfer the shape to your full-sized sheet. Dry and press the paper as desired.

Moonscape

The success of this sheet depends on finding the right paper for recycling. You want paper that is heavily clay-coated and shiny, with huge expanses of deep-colored ink. Heavy clay coating is identified by a high gloss; it's a very shiny paper. Not all shiny paper uses clay, though, so look for the glossiest and shiniest piece you can find. Magazine covers and interior pages are good hunting grounds, as are slick advertising pieces.

You'll know you've succeeded if you get a lot of foam while blending the paper. Foam indicates a clay formula coating, and it is the key to the bubble effect you want as the finished result. When you pour the foamy pulp into the deckle, the foam bubbles start bursting. Each burst sprays out minute clay particles, colored by the ink. The bigger the bubbles, the more obvious the effect. For the best result, aim to keep the bubbles intact until they are down near the screen. When the conditions are right, a quite spectacular visual surface can be made.

Step 1. Prepare your mold and lower it into the vat (*see step 3, page 53*) before blending the pulp. Leave it there while you run the blender.

Step 2. Add the shiny paper and water to the blender. Run it for about 12 to 15 seconds on a low speed, then turn the blender up to high speed. There should be some foam generated.

Step 3. Turn the blender off, pour the recycled pulp into the hand mold, and lift the mold out of the water as rapidly as possible. You want the least amount of foam bubbles to dissipate before the pulp has drained down onto the screen. In the best case, many small bubbles and a number of large ones will burst *as the pulp reaches the screen.*

Step 4. Complete the steps for making paper, as usual.

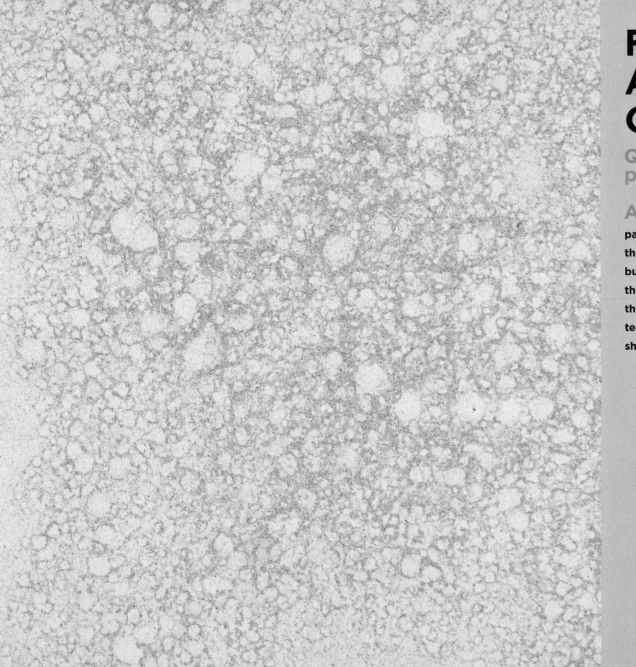

Frequently Asked Questions

Q: Can I recycle shiny paper?

A: Yes, you most certainly can. What makes shiny paper shine is a coating of clay. When you recycle the paper, there will be a lot of foam in the blender, but that is no problem. In fact, the clay used at the paper mill is very expensive and is not a bad thing for your handmade sheet. The moonscape technique shows what shiny paper can do that non-shiny papers can't.

Texturing

The wet surface of a newly formed sheet is easily textured — the wetter, the better. Any textured surface put down on a wet sheet will impact the position of the fibers. This opens more worlds than one mind can conquer. Think about all the cloth surfaces in a large fabric store, from canvas to netting. Each can be used to texture a newly formed sheet of paper. There are plenty of nonfabric surfaces out there, too, so keep your eyes open as you move through your day.

Fine Texture

Step 1. Choose a piece of cloth with a very fine weave, such as bed sheeting, and cut close to the size of the paper sheet you're texturing.

Step 2. Make a full-sized sheet of paper, following the basic papermaking procedure through step 6 (*see page 54*), but don't put on the cover screen. Instead, lay the fabric over the new paper sheet and apply the sponge to remove some water. Leave the fabric on the sheet throughout all the remaining papermaking steps.

Step 3. Remove the piece of bed sheet carefully after the paper sheet dries. Examine the paper sheet's surface closely and move your fingertips across it to feel the texture.

Coarse Texture

Step 1. Choose a piece of cloth with a pronounced, rough, dimensional surface. Perhaps you can find cloth that is ribbed, such as corduroy. Cut a piece close to the size of the paper sheet you're texturing.

Step 2. Repeat Steps 2 and 3 in the previous section.

The colored strips were textured by the grout pattern on the back of a ceramic tile (shown underneath), then pulp-layered onto the surface of a white sheet of paper.

Embossing

A good subject for spirited debate over coffee would be, "Where does texturing end and embossing begin?" They are similar in that both impact the surface of handmade paper, but embossing raises or lowers the surface in a particular shape or pattern, beyond what would be considered the paper's normal surface. You could think of embossing as exaggerated texturing, and it does indeed add a fresh dimension to paper. In commercial papers, embossing is often done to paper after it is manufactured. Here is a way to do it as the paper is made.

Step 1. Select a rough or patterned surface to use as an embossing plate. Prepare the pulp and make a full-sized sheet of paper, following the basic papermaking procedure through step 6 (*see page 54*), but don't put on the cover screen.

Step 2. Place the embossing plate on the surface of the newly formed wet sheet. Carefully press down on the plate, observing how the new sheet's pulp rises into the embossing plate's open areas.

Step 3. Put the cover screen over the new sheet and embossing plate. Leave the embossing plate in place as you continue making the paper. Handle the sheet carefully, because any shifting of the embossing plate will distort the embossing.

Step 4. Replace the top and bottom wet couch sheets with dry ones before pressing the sheet. With the embossing plate still in place, put the new sheet and couch sheets under pressure in a press or under weight of any kind.

Step 5. Remove the dry sheet carefully, followed by the embossing piece. This should result in an excellently embossed sheet.

Crafty Tip

Craft stores offer a great number of metal embossing plates, as well as plastic stencils, many of which can be used for embossing handmade paper as it is being made. Also consider using small, reasonably flat jewelry or other such items you might find around the house and apply them in the same ways as you would an embossing plate. You also can find embossed felts at most craft stores. Instead of a cover screen, put an embossed felt over a newly formed sheet and leave it on through final drying.

*This larger embossing plate can produce
a nice facing for a greeting card.*

Screen Block Out: Windows

In papermaking, where the water goes, the fiber goes. Consequently, if you block off part of your screen's surface, the water won't go there and neither will the fibers. If you want to make a sheet half the size of your hand mold, simply cover half your screen with a solid material. If you want an open space in the middle, place some solid material (such as thin wood, foam core, or plastic) cut to the size and shape you desire in the middle of your screen. It's another world to explore.

Step 1. Cut out an image from a foam food tray or a thin board (*see page 80*). For your first experiment, try something easy like a heart, square, or other simple shape. The size must be smaller than the papermaking screen.

Step 2. Blend the pulp and set the assembled mold into the water. Place the cut-out image on the screen wherever you wish. Hold it down firmly, so no pulp will run under it.

Step 3. Pour the pulp into the deckle using your other hand. If this gets too difficult, ask someone to help you, especially in the next step.

Step 4. Keep the image firmly on the screen while lifting the hand mold out of the water. Hold it level while the water drains.

Step 5. Remove the paper and screen from the mold and set them on a drain pan.

Let water drain for several minutes. Carefully remove the cut-out shape from the screen. Take care that the pulp around the edges of the image doesn't rise with the image. If you used a foam food tray, you can insert a pin at a slant into the image to help lift it.

Step 6. Lower a cover screen over the new sheet and complete the papermaking process.

Planning Ahead

If you like to make greeting cards, think about how the placement of an opening might work in your favor. For instance, when the paper is folded in half, a shaped opening in front might become a window for words or images inside the card.

Super 3-D Window Card

This project uses the screen block out technique described on the previous page. Use the finished book as a child's toy, and add words to make it a book about shapes. Or use it as a greeting card or art gift for an adult.

Materials

- Papermaking supplies (*see page 25*)
- Square molds, about 5" square (*see* Tip)
- Cookie cutters or pie-tin molds (*see pages 80–81*) for interior shapes
- Clear tape or needle and thread for joining pages

Instructions

1. As described on the previous page, place the cookie cutter directly in the center of the mold and pour the pulp. Do this for each page, each time with a different shape, in a nice variety of colors.

2. Blot and dry the papers.

3. If keeping the rough edges, attach the pages along the sides using tape. If trimming the edges, you can stitch them together with needle and thread instead. Stitching works better on cut edges, as the thread can catch on rough edges.

Crafty Tip

Square molds can be made from old picture frames with the glass and backing removed, or square containers such as milk cartons. Or you can wing it by setting up four sponges in a square shape. Whatever will hold the pulp in place is fair game!

Joined by invisible tape, sheets with assorted windows can make a surprising accordion-fold book.

Deckle Division

Deckle division is simply dividing your hand mold's deckle into two or more compartments. In an undivided deckle, you can pour only one kind or color of pulp. In a deckle divided into two separate compartments, you can pour in two kinds of colors of pulp, one in each compartment. If you remove the divider while the two pulps are draining (after the mold is lifted from the water), the two pulps will flow into each other. This can produce dramatic effects, resulting in a single sheet made of two different pulps.

For the deckle divider, use a piece of foam core or cut what you need from a piece of foam food board (the kind meat or pastries are packaged on). Measure and cut it to fit snugly inside the deckle as shown. Once you've prepared the deckle divider, the rest is easy.

Dividing the deckle is not hard, yet it opens wide many doors to creativity and unusual, striking handmade sheets.

Step 1. Blend two different pulp colors, one at a time, and pour them into separate containers.

Step 2. Slide the divided deckle into the vat. Gently pour one pulp into half of the deckle and the second pulp into the other half. Agitate the pulp gently in both compartments.

Step 3. Lift the mold up and out of the water with one hand. When ¼ to ½ of the deckle's pulp has drained, use your other

hand to quickly pull the foam divider straight up and out. The portions of the pulps not drained will flow into each other, forming a single sheet.

Step 4. Allow all the water to drain out and complete the papermaking process as usual.

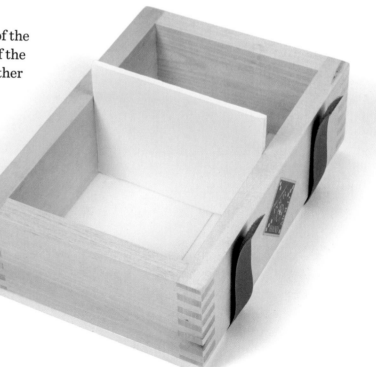

Crafty Tips

○ Pulps can sometimes be made to flow into each other more forcefully by gently rocking the mold after the divider has been lifted. This can create more dramatic sheets. Experiment.

○ If you are unable to lift the hand mold with one hand, get someone to help; or lift the mold and set it quickly on a surface and then lift the divider.

○ This technique will produce a two-sided sheet. On one side, the line where the two pulps meet will be indistinct or almost nonexistent (*above*). On the other, it will likely be sharply defined (*at right*).

Sheet Layering

This technique has almost everything in common with pulp layering (*see page 78*), except here you are dealing with an entire sheet. This requires adept, more careful handling, but sheet layering offers its own effects, including two-sided sheets. This is also a good technique to remember when it's necessary to patch a very weak sheet or a sheet with thin spots or holes in it. It is another field that offers a great deal of exploration. The basic introduction that follows can get you started on your own unique experiments.

Step 1. Prepare white pulp and make a sheet of paper through step 5 (*see page 54*), but don't put the cover screen on the new sheet. Set aside the sheet to drain.

Step 2. Prepare colored pulp and make a second thin sheet of paper. When you lift the screen and colored sheet from the mold, drag it screen-side-down over a wrung-out sponge to pull some of the water out of the

sheet. Then, turn the screen over so the colored sheet is on the bottom side. The sheet is not likely to fall from the screen unless it is exceedingly wet or very thick.

Step 3. Lower the colored sheet down onto the white one, perfectly matching the edges of the two sheets. (Yes, perfectly matching the edges is difficult; just give it your best shot.)

Step 4. Complete the papermaking process as usual. The result will be a sheet that is white on one side and colored on the other. In future experiments, combine any two types of sheets you think would be exciting.

Simple foldouts are an easy and dramatic way to use sheet-layered paper. The cutout can be made from any symmetrical shape. Just trace half of the shape anywhere on the front of the folded sheet layered paper, and make a dotted line from top to bottom down the middle of your shape. Cut along the traced line, and score and fold along the dotted line. (See the template on page 199.)

How to Make Cards That Sell

Few people are as productive as Maria Nerius, an author, editor, papermaker, craft industry consultant, media hostess, and more. Having once made crafts for a living, Maria paid attention to how things sold. She spends much of her professional life encouraging designers and crafters to learn how to make money on their crafts. Here's her short list for making cards that sell:

- O You can have the cutest cards in town, but if you're using unpopular colors, the cards will not sell. Make paper and cards with current color trends! A trip to the card or gift shop can inspire fresh, innovative ideas.

- O Make a professional presentation. Display cards in clear, plastic sleeves. Make prices clear with stickers or signage.

- O Offer a quantity discount. If you sell one for $2.95, offering four for $10 often nets the $10 purchase.

- O Make cards people need. Popular card categories are birthday, wedding, baby, and thank you.

You're Invited!

For some fun invitations or thank you notes, try this simple design. Use the template on page 200 to make your own template out of food board (for instructions, *see page 80*). When the paper is dry, write a personal message and fold on the lines shown on the template (folded cards will be 3½" × 5"). Seal and mail with a first class stamp, or send in a larger self-sealing envelope.

Watermarking

Sometimes, when paper is held up to light, an image can be seen in the paper. This image is a watermark, a spot where the paper is thinner and more light can pass through. If you can make your paper thinner in selected areas, you can make a watermark.

Watermarks have a fascinating history. They have been an item of mystique since 1282 and are still used for identification, authentication, anti-counterfeit,

anti-fraud, and artistic expression. Commercially, watermark technology can be pretty advanced, producing complex watermarks that appear shaded and dimensional like a photograph. A look-alike watermark can be added chemically after the paper is dry.

Fortunately for home papermakers, there's also effective primitive technology for making watermarks. Bend a wire into an image, or form an image with something flat and not too broad. Secure it to the face of a papermaking screen and make a sheet. Where the image was on the screen, the paper will be thinner. When held to the light, the watermark will be revealed.

Two Toothpicks

This is a simple exercise in watermarking, though it can deliver a delightful and clear mark. Primarily, it gives you the sense of how the first mark was sewn onto the face of a papermaking screen. The materials are easy to get and easy to use.

Step 1. Assemble some flat toothpicks, a needle and thread, and a piece of window screen as big as your papermaking screen. The window screen is suggested because you might not want to use your papermaking screen for your first effort.

Step 2. Arrange the toothpicks on the surface of the window screen in a simple design; for instance, the form of a V. With the needle and thread, tack the toothpicks to the screen, rather than sewing along their entire length. A tack at each end and one in the middle should suffice.

Step 3. Following the basic hand papermaking steps (*see page 52*), make a sheet of paper, using the window screen as the papermaking screen. Take care when removing the sheet from the screen. When the sheet is dry, hold it to the light and behold your watermark.

Plastic Letters

For a more complex watermark, try forming a message in your paper. "Smile" is easy for a first effort. A personal favorite is "Don't Panic." We went with "Top Secret!" Choose some ½"-tall plastic, self-adhesive letters from an office supply store. When using thicker letters, the paper you make will need to be thick enough so the letters won't break the surface. The idea is to experiment to find what works — and don't forget to have fun!

Step 1. Apply the letters to the face of the papermaking screen, leaving ¼" between them. Will the letters stick? Usually. Roll over them with a rolling pin after they are on the screen. How long will they stay after being dunked in water? I've had varying luck, with some sticking for a long time and others a short time.

Step 2. Follow the basic papermaking steps (*see page 52*), using the screen with the watermark to make a sheet of paper. Be aware that paper thickness is of great

importance when using plastic letters for a watermark. If the paper's too thick, the mark doesn't show. If too thin, the mark makes a hole in the paper. Keep adjusting the amount of pulp until the thickness is right. Then, write down your formula for future use.

Crafty Tips

○ You can use contact cement in addition to (or instead of) needle and thread. It can be messy, though, so use sparingly. If cement fills any screen pores to either side of the toothpicks, the water flow through the screen will be affected, to the detriment of the watermark.

○ If the watermark in the final sheet is too obvious, make the next sheet a little thicker. If it is too dim or hard to see, make the next sheet thinner.

○ For a more complex, custom watermark, try forming your own designs with bent wire. A humble plastic twist-tie can be effective, or use something else that is easy to bend, such as coiled solder. Use needle nose pliers to shape the latter. Coiled solder is so malleable it can be bent around images, such as cookie cutters, to form shapes.

Board Drying

As you can well imagine, the way you dry your paper can affect what the paper surface looks like. Board drying is a very old technique, practiced by early Chinese papermakers. The surface used in this technique need not be a board. It can be any water-safe surface that appeals to you. It's a good idea to spray the surface before you start, to lessen release problems. You can use silicone (read the label about good ventilation), cooking sprays, or petroleum jelly. Keep the coverage light, though, and wipe off all excess release aid before applying the sheet.

Step 1. Select a board or other flat surface at least 2" longer and wider than the paper sheet you're making. Make sure the surface is clean.

Step 2. Prepare pulp and make a sheet of handmade paper through step 5 (*see page 54*). Allow water to drain naturally from the sheet for 2 minutes. This will provide some stabilization of the sheet.

Step 3. Pick up the new sheet and screen and turn them over. Gently put the new sheet down onto the board's surface. Use a sponge, couch sheet, and press bar as usual to pull as much water out of the sheet as possible.

Step 4. Peel off the couch sheet carefully. Leave the new paper sheet in place until it is dry, then remove it from the board. If you have trouble lifting the dry sheet off the board, try working it off by inserting a knife blade between the sheet and the board at various places around the sheet. Then continue to lift gently.

Bored? Try a Board!

Board drying can deliver an amazing surprise. When I saw a board with a knot on its surface, I decided I wanted to reproduce the knot's texture-swirls on a sheet of paper. I carried out the process of board drying, placing the wet sheet over the knot. But, when I took off the dry sheet expecting to see texturing, what I actually saw was a meticulously detailed and accurate reproduction of the knot — in full, gorgeous, true color.

This was a whole new world to explore! I tried more board surface knots. Another surprise: Not one of them was reproduced on my paper. This made my first lucky result even more valued. Will it ever happen again? The hunt must continue. Perhaps the "right" board has to be found, one not overly cured and certainly without any finish. The situation needs further exploration. Join me. Beat me to another successful sheet.

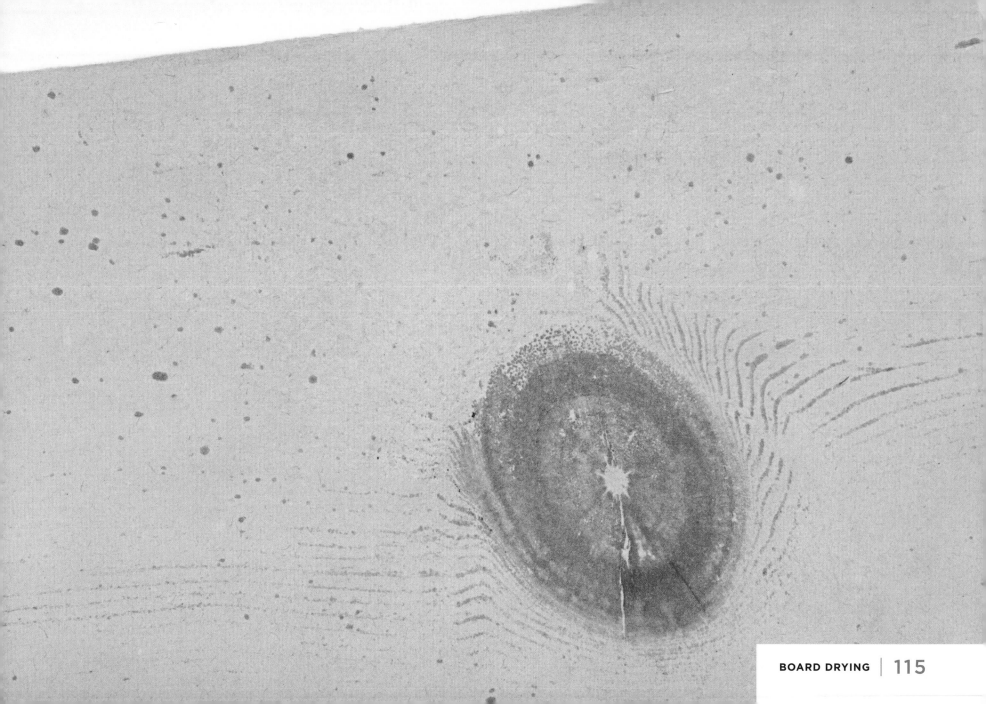

Air Drying

Air drying produces a soft sheet with a variegated surface. From an art standpoint, the surface produced by unfettered shrinkage forces can be highly dramatic. The precise nature of the air-dried surface can vary widely, depending on the pulps used for the sheet, the rate of drying (high or low relative humidity), and whether any type of restraint is placed on the surface during drying.

Left totally unrestrained, pulp shrinkage can result in a sheet that might be relatively flat or extremely curled. Almost always, the surface will not be very smooth. Sometimes, sheet flatness can be maintained by putting weights on either end of the papermaking screen during drying. A window screen or very light cloth can be placed over the sheet and kept taut but relaxed with weights at either end. As with most techniques, air drying is a great field for experimentation.

Step 1. Prepare pulp and make a sheet of handmade paper through step 5 (*see page 54*).

Step 2. Set the papermaking screen, with the wet sheet on it, somewhere to dry. Allow it to dry solely by evaporation. To help speed things up, the screen and sheet can be pulled across the surface of a wrung-out sponge to remove some water, and the sheet can be set on or near a drying force, such as a heat register or a sunny window.

Rugged and untamed, this surface of an air dried, pulp-painted sheet shows the power of unrestrained shrinkage forces.

Air Plus Pressure

A combination of air and press drying creates a cameo, textured image area on an otherwise smooth surface, creating dimension, kind of like embossing in reverse. One procedure is described below; variations will likely occur to you after trying this project.

Try It

Step 1. Locate a foam food tray or piece of wood larger than the sheet of paper you're making. Cut an image (tree, animal, heart) into the material that will be an open space for air drying.

Step 2. Prepare pulp and make a sheet of handmade paper through step 5 (*see page 54*). Remove the papermaking screen and new sheet from the hand mold and place them on a drain rack or smooth surface. For experimentation, try adding a bit more pulp, possibly of another color, in the area where the cut-out image will be.

Step 3. Place the foam tray or wood carefully on top of the new sheet. Press down slowly and uniformly. The board will compress the covered part of the sheet, while leaving the cut-out image area at the original height.

Step 4. Turn the assembled pieces (foam or wood, new sheet, screen) upside down, so the foam or wood is on the bottom and the screen on the top. Remove water from the sheet by pressing on the screen with a sponge.

Step 5. Remove the papermaking screen carefully and replace it with a couch sheet. Press down on the couch sheet until it has removed all the water it can, carefully remove it, and replace it with a dry one. When removing a wet couch sheet, the paper sheet might tend to rise with it. Use your fingernail or a knife to keep that from happening.

Step 6. Turn the whole package over again, so the couch sheet is on the bottom and the foam or wood on top. Place a weight (book, container of water, brick) on the foam or wood board to provide pressure. Change the couch sheet as it gets damp until the paper sheet is dry. In the finished sheet, the part that was dried under pressure will have a smooth surface, and the air-dried cutout will be rough.

Variation

For another effect, you can make a sheet as usual, remove it from the deckle, and do the following:

O Put a cover screen over half of it and sponge only the half covered by the cover screen.

O Remove the cover screen, put couch sheets over only that half, and put pressure for drying only on the couch sheets, permitting the other half of the sheet to air dry.

O Change couch sheets as they get damp until the sheet is dry.

Bonded for Life

Another favorite project involves the self-bonding technique. No glue, tape, or adhesive is used to hold the pages of this book together.

Materials

O   **Papermaking supplies** (*see page 25*)

Instructions

1. Use tin cans, shapes, or a standard hand mold to make a sheet of paper in the usual way.

2. Remove water so the sheet holds together but is still reasonably damp. Transfer to couch material. Lay a couch sheet or cloth on the newly formed sheet, leaving a ¾″ border of paper exposed on the left edge.

3. Make a second sheet. Remove enough water so the paper can be handled but is still damp. Lay the second paper directly over first. On the left edge where damp sheets meet, the pages will self-bond. Use a spray bottle to lightly mist and re-wet this area. Separated by the couch material, the rest of the sheet will become an open page for the book.

4. Continue to make and layer sheets, as described in step 3.

5. Use as much pressure as possible to press the stack of sheets with couch material.

6. Change couch sheets as needed until the papers (your new book) are dry. If the handmade paper is thicker than standard text weight, there is no need for front and back covers.

The sheets shown here are
naturally bonded in the
papermaking process.

Chapter 7
Paper Casting

In paper casting, you reproduce a shape by pressing malleable pulp onto that shape and leaving it to dry.

Think of lining the inside or outside of an ice cream cone with wet plaster and letting it dry. The plaster will dry in the shape of the cone. Wet pulp behaves similarly. The same pulp that makes a flat sheet of paper can become a three-dimensional shape.

Laying the Foundation

Because papermaking fibers are microscopic, wet pulp can be worked into or onto a surface's most minute details and crevices, which are then reproduced when allowed to dry. Consequently, wet pulp is an ideal medium for casting.

Most of what you need for paper casting is the same as for flat papermaking (*see page 25*). The primary differences are the molds you use, the type of fibers you need for pulp, and any special additives and release agents. All are covered in this chapter.

Molds

Commercial casting molds are available in three types: plastic, flexible, and rigid.

Plastic.
Cookie stamps, soap and candy molds, and many other kinds of plastic crafting molds have interesting detail that will emboss the surface of the finished cast. Hundreds of designs are available in plastic, varying in size from a few inches (candy molds) to a few feet (cement stepping stone molds). Since this plastic has such a hard, shiny surface, the dried cast separates easily from the mold with few problems. Unfortunately, most plastic molds lack surface detail, which may be a disadvantage.

Flexible.
Flexible molds are good for three-dimensional pieces of art because they are strong and elastic. Polymer clay casting molds are an example of a flexible mold. However, because cotton linters and recycled papers start out as such a watery medium, flexible molds can be difficult to use. Pressing to remove water and encourage bonding is difficult.

Rigid.
Rigid molds are made of fired clay or composite resins. They come in many sizes and shapes, and have multipurpose uses. The same mold might be used for paper casting, cookie or butter stamping, metal embossing, or casting of various products to make jewelry. Rigid molds are generally the most desirable molds for paper casting. They accommodate water and lots of pressing and patting, and further have fine detail and depth. With care, rigid molds can be used over and over and will produce a clear, interesting finished product, ready for various art applications and useful gift projects.

Unglazed ceramic molds are the traditional choice for paper casting molds. The absorbent nature of fired clay draws water into the mold, bringing fibers along into the details and crevices of the image for a superlative cast.

Shown are just a few possible options to use as casting molds:

- **A** *plastic push molds for polymer clay*
- **B** *antique brass plate (found object)*
- **C** *glass candle diffuser from a dollar store*
- **D** *textured metal picture frame (see page 136)*
- **E** *commercial terra cotta casting mold*
- **F** *commercial bisque clay casting mold*
- **G** *metal wall art (see page 124)*

Frequently Asked Questions

Q: Will plastic candy molds work for paper casting?

A: Most paper-casting molds (*see previous page*) are made from kiln-fired clay. Clay molds pull water, and fibers with it, into the details of the mold, producing high-resolution results. Plastic molds generally won't deliver the detail one anticipates. Applying linter or recycled fiber to a nonporous surface encourages formation of air bubbles between the mold and pressed-in pulp. Pock marks may appear on the cast's surface. If you have some candy molds at home, by all means try them out. If you find the results suitable, the variety of inexpensive plastic molds outweighs any concern.

Casting with Everyday Objects

Paper casting is a limitless world in which your imagination can roam endlessly, and your decorative and artistic senses can find a thousand paths to pursue. There are certainly some everyday things around the house, or maybe your grandmother's attic, that can be used for paper casting. Keep an eye on the amazing and functional shapes and forms found in fast-food restaurants, ice cream parlors, and grocery stores. There are neat tray and small-box forms everywhere. A round shape is universally pleasing and can be useful as well.

Set a glass or similar round object in the middle of a larger round pulp patty (*see page 132*). With a plastic spatula, push the pulp patty's edges up around the bottom of the glass, let the pulp dry, and you get all types of coasterlike creations. Spray them with clear polyurethane (*see page 127*), and they will develop moisture resistance. You also can do your own thing freehand with a turkey baster as a drawing or forming tool. Through surface embedment (*see page 64*), you can celebrate and immortalize contemporary entertainment and commercial icons, a memento from your kid's card games, or the graduation card of a grandchild.

Pulp

As with other papermaking, any fiber — new or out of your wastebasket — can be used for paper casting. The resources in your wastebasket will give you a broad range of colors and hues that are free. Professionally dyed colored pulp is abundant and free in the form of throw-away colored paper.

Cotton linters have become the "fiber of choice" for paper casting, and the preference is easily explained. Cotton linters sold for casting have been appropriately "beaten." This process modifies the fiber by shortening it. Short fibers are most desirable for casting because they can enter the casting's most minute detail.

Linters' exceptional whiteness allows the eye to see dimension and shadow on the finished cast. The shrinkage rate of the drying pulp is very low, preserving both detail and proportion of the mold. Cotton linters, in terms of an art medium, are economical. These qualities and their exceptional replication of detail provide the characteristics most desired in pulp for paper casting.

Paper Casting Tips

○ Are you using recycled pulp? A general guideline for the ratio of wastepaper to water is a torn-up 8½" × 11" sheet of paper to 3 cups of water. Run the blender until chunks of paper are no longer visible.

○ Regardless of what pulp is used (cotton linter or recycled paper), the good news is that both can be processed in a kitchen blender. Should a paper casting fail to turn out for any reason, reblend it. Linters can always be redispersed in a blender for another attempt or project.

Preshredded cotton linters

Cotton linter squares

Cotton linters are available in four forms: sheet pulp, perforated squares, preshredded bulk, and liquid pulp. Some are easier to use and some are less expensive, but every form delivers the beautiful results.

Cotton linter sheets. This is the most economical form of cotton linter. For best results and long life for your blender, reduce to 2″ pieces, presoak for several minutes, and then put in a blender with 3 to 4 cups of water. Never blend more than the equivalent of a 5″ × 7″ section in the blender.

Cotton linter squares. Cotton linter squares are easy to use, especially for beginning paper casting. Sheets are perforated into 1″ squares, making it easy to premeasure pulp. The number of squares it takes to cover the mold's image is the right amount to use. Never blend more than 36 squares at a time.

Preshredded cotton linters. Preshredded cotton linter has the advantage of being very blender friendly. Never exceed 1 cup of linter in the blender at a time.

Liquid pulp. Cotton linter pulp that has been beaten and blended is available by the bucket and can be ordered and shipped from specific vendors (*see* Resources, *page 196*). Liquid pulp can be ordered with sizing or other additives included. Follow the directions from the supplier for use and storage tips.

Frequently Asked Questions

Q: My ceramic mold is stained from some colored pulp I used. Is it ruined?

A: No, your mold isn't ruined. Set the mold on paper toweling. Spritz the mold with a solution of 50 percent water and 50 percent bleach. The bleach water will be absorbed into the clay and neutralize color in the stain. It won't make the stain disappear, but it *usually* prevents future casts from picking up the stain color.

Simple Tints for Cotton Linters

Linters are a wonderful fiber source for paper casting, because the fibers easily form a strong, natural bond. When the water is drained away from the mass of wet fibers, the mass is already forming a workable pulp that can be handled easily. The shrinkage rate of the drying pulp is very low, which helps preserve the detail of the mold.

O Although a bright white cotton linter cast is traditional and often preferable, many individuals like to add color to pulp.

O Do try: Adding small pieces of gift wrap tissue, napkins, or colorful paper to linters in the blender until the desired hue is reached.

O Not recommended: Construction paper (messy and ineffective since dye bleeds into the water and stains molds, sponges, and toweling), food coloring (ineffective and permanent staining similar to construction paper), and acrylic paints (both ineffective and foamy in the blender).

Additives

A variety of additives can be used in casting pulp. These are said to yield firmer casting surfaces that are more suitable for painting and to provide other characteristics. Anything put into pulp will have some kind of effect, subtle or obvious. Here are just a few of many options you might try. Be sure you get instructions and any expiration information from your vendor. If they produce a discernible effect on your casting, that's good. If not, don't waste your money.

Wax sizing.
Many bleached-white bakery sacks are made of heavily waxed paper. Adding some of this paper to cotton linters or other pulp for casting delivers wax sizing to the casting. The more waxed paper added, the harder the surface. The sizing factor prevents feathering and wicking of liquid paints and inks.

Methylcellulose.
This sizing agent has mixed reviews for use in castings. Besides providing sizing (*see page 33*), it is also an adhesive and can cause release problems for a casting. Follow supplier recommendations and use a release agent.

Commercial sizes.
Internal sizing is the addition of sizing to pulp *before* product formation, while external sizing is the addition *after* product formation.

Calcium carbonate.
This hard (ground limestone) filler lends some surface hardness and permanency (meaning the casting will last longer). Some of what is added will be deposited at the surface of a casting.

Papermaker's clay.
The state of Georgia is slowly disappearing into paper, because it is a prime source of kaolin clay. The clay works in a similar way as calcium carbonate, but without affecting permanency. It may give paper casts a grayish tinge.

External polyurethane spray.
Spraying clear polyurethane lightly on the face of a cotton linter paper casting can result in a very closed, hard-sized, and firm surface. But addition of anything will result in some loss of brightness. Experiment on small, easy-to-make castings to test results with a particular art medium.

Release Agents

Sometimes, when trying to pull or lift a dry casting from its mold, part or much of the casting sticks to the surface. The casting does not release. If a paper casting shows signs of not releasing, try slipping a thin blade under the casting at some place along its edge and proceed with a delicate touch to lift and pry the cast loose. The same cotton linters that release satisfactorily *without* additives might present more of a release problem *with* additives or tinting materials. Severe sticking is unfortunately a harbinger of a paper casting fatality.

Often, a release agent can prevent sticking by facilitating a dry casting to release easily and completely. A release agent is applied to the mold's surface prior to applying pulp.

Common Release Agents

Silicon spray is easily available, is mostly inorganic, and is least invasive of both the paper and mold. It is easily applied and minimally messy. Read all safety comments on the packaging; you may prefer not to allow children to use it. Below are some other options.

- Nonstick vegetable spray
- Mold release spray
- Glycerin
- Paste wax
- Petroleum jelly (can be diluted with mineral spirits)

Whichever agent you use, observe safety practices as described on the labels. Use the least amount of release agent possible. No puddles should be visible. A light wipe with an absorbent material will eliminate excess.

The vintage cookie mold shown on the previous page was used to produce this paper casting.

Frequently Asked Questions

Q: Even after I apply release agent, I'm still having a sticking problem. What's wrong?

A: Sometimes, small fibers are caught in a detail of the mold. They try to bond with the next round of pulp in the mold and cause sticking or "pocking" on the surface of the cast. To avoid this problem, use a stiff brush to clean the mold and reapply the release agent. Serious sticking in ceramic molds requires boiling the mold in hot water for 10 minutes. Experience has shown this works every time.

Q: Can I use a microwave to dry a paper cast?

A: Not all molds can withstand microwave heat. Ram-pressed ceramic molds are generally fired at a high enough temperature to prevent breakage. Even so, there's a chance a small air pocket in the clay will fill with water and expand during microwaving, causing the mold to crack or explode. Check manufacturer guidelines regarding microwave safety. If in doubt whether the mold will hold up, avoid microwave drying.

1. Put the microwave on a medium setting.

2. Microwave the ceramic mold and cast for 1 minute.

3. Give the mold a quarter turn.

4. Microwave for 30 seconds.

5. Repeat steps 3 and 4 until dry. Many casts will dry in 2 minutes. If the cast is still damp, peel it from mold and finish with air drying.

Caution: The mold will be hot from microwaving, so take care when handling. Also, prolonged microwaving can cause scorching.

How to Make a Paper Cast

The basic steps for paper casting are very simple. Try this warm-up exercise to whet your appetite.

Instructions

Step 1. Tear off enough cotton linter casting squares, other cotton linters, or six thicknesses of wastepaper (enough to cover the selected mold).

Step 2. Put the linters or wastepaper in the blender with 3 cups of water. Blend on low for several seconds, then on high for 45 seconds.

Step 3. Pour the blender's contents (pulp) into the tea strainer. Let the water drain into the measuring cup.

Step 4. Plop the pulp directly from the strainer onto the mold. Jiggle the pulp gently with your hand, shaking the fibers into the mold's details. Maintain uniform thickness as much as possible.

Step 5. Hold the cast over the measuring cup or a sink and press firmly with your hand to settle the pulp and squeeze out

Materials

- Cotton linter or selected wastepaper
- Kitchen blender
- Water
- 4-cup measuring glass
- Tea strainer or wire mesh
- Casting mold
- Sponge
- Toweling, terrycloth, or paper towels

the water. When the casting is no longer dripping wet, set it on a flat surface and continue pressing with a sponge to remove more water.

Step 6. Finish up by pressing with a terrycloth or paper towel to remove as much moisture as possible.

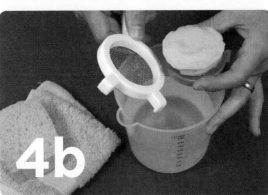

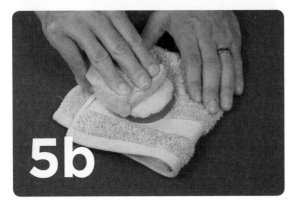

Drying a Cast

For final drying, there are four options:

1. Peel the cast carefully from the mold and let it air dry.

2. Place the cast on the mold in front of a fan or heating vent to speed drying.

3. If the mold you're using can withstand heat, leave the cast on the mold and place it in a 275°F oven. Check it after 10 minutes; drying time depends on cast thickness. Usually, the casting will start to lift from the mold when dry.

4. If the mold is microwave-safe (check the manufacturer's guidelines), follow the steps in the box on page 129.

Application Methods

Putting pulp on a small mold is quite easy. On bigger molds, bowls, carvings, or other objects, applying pulp can be a bit more of an undertaking. Below is a range of ways to apply pulp; just remember that it's best to apply a release agent to the mold before applying pulp.

Pulp Pull-Away

An easy way to get pulp onto a flat mold is to pour pulp from a blender into a strainer and let the water drain into a pail or bowl.

When the pulp is thick enough to handle (*see* Handling Pulp, *next page*), pull chunks of pulp from the strainer and layer them evenly across the surface of the mold. Pat pieces together to form a uniform layer before removing any water.

Pulp Transfer

A more efficient way to move larger amounts of pulp to a flat mold is sometimes needed. Pour the wet pulp into a strainer and shake it back and forth, making the

water drain rapidly and forming the pulp into an oval ball. This can be plopped directly onto the surface of a mold. Repeat until the mold is covered. Pat all sections together to form a uniform layer before removing any water.

Pulp Patties

Making a cast on the surface of bowls or trays may require yet another process for transferring pulp. Pulp patties are one way to arrange pulp on large, uneven, round, or

Laying pulp pieces onto a mold.

Transferring pulp onto a mold directly from a strainer.

Flattening a pulp patty.

curved surfaces. Merging patties of diverse colorful pulps is another benefit.

Pour the pulp from the blender into the strainer, letting water drain into a pail or bowl. Now, dump the pulp on any flat surface. With your hands, flatten the pulp into a patty of reasonably uniform thickness; patting it with a firm bristled brush is helpful. Remove water with a sponge, and if necessary, with a terrycloth towel, until the pulp patty can be handled. Finally, place the patty on the mold. Repeat, overlapping colors and wetting patty edges until the container is covered.

Handling Pulp

Casting often involves handling pulp, laying sections or strips on a mold, and pressing them together into a larger form or shape. The challenge is to remove sufficient water so pulp can be handled, but not so much that adjacent sections or strips won't bond with each other. Make it a goal to remove no more water than is necessary. Rewet adjacent pulp pieces and sheet edges after application to the mold. Press with a sponge. By doing this, you will restrengthen the bond between individual pieces or sections of pulp.

Easy Bowl

Find a kitchen bowl with a pleasing shape and apply a release agent. Mix a few different colors in plastic cups and press the pulp into place as you like. The water may pool a bit in this method, but carefully blot with a paper towel and allow to air dry as needed.

Fingers are a good way to work different pulps together into a single cohesive mass.

Materials

- Cotton linter or selected wastepaper
- Kitchen blender
- Water
- 4-cup measuring glass
- Tea strainer or wire mesh
- Casting mold
- Sponge
- Toweling, terrycloth, or paper towels

Making Pulp Strips for Casting

Applying strips of pulp made from recycled paper is another way to arrange pulp on flat molds or everyday objects. Use several colors, if you wish.

Materials

- 18" square fine mesh hardware cloth
- Bucket, tub, or tray
- 18" square window screen
- Two wood 1" × 2" × 12" boards
- Pulp (amount depends on how many strips are being made)
- Plastic pitcher or turkey baster or squeeze bottle
- Sponge, terrycloth, or paper towels

Instructions

Step 1. Put the hardware screen over the bucket or tray, then place the window screen over the hardware cloth.

Step 2. Place two boards beside each other on the screen, as far apart as you want the strip or sheet to be wide. *Note:* you can also make wedge shapes, handy for making paper casts of bowls.

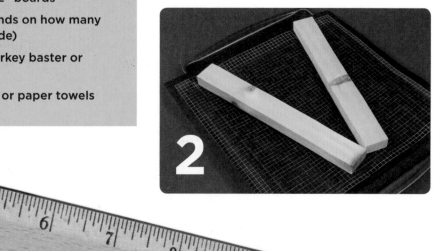

Step 3. Pour or squeeze pulp slowly onto the screen between the boards, to whatever depth desired.

Step 4. Wait for the pulp to drain and then remove the boards.

Step 5. Use a sponge, terrycloth, or paper toweling to remove water from the strips or sheets to a point where they can be handled and applied to a surface or mold.

a

b

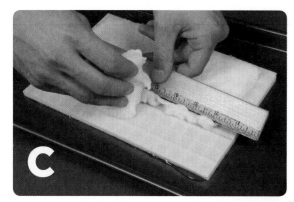

c

Pulp Sheets and Strips Made with a Deckle

A pour hand mold can be useful for paper casting. A uniform layer of recycled fiber or cotton linter pulp is easily achieved, and that saves a lot of time and effort. Follow the usual steps for papermaking, but increase the amount of recycled fiber to get a thicker pulp layer for casting.

Strips can be torn or pulled from a sheet with the help of a ruler (c) and layered on a mold. They can be laid across the mold, each slightly overlapping the preceding one, until the mold is covered. A second layer can be added at right angles to the first. Strips are an excellent way to build up a paper casting's thickness.

Holding It All Together

When you cast using strips, a weak spot exists where one strip meets another. Fiber batches do not bond strongly where they touch. Here are some ways to address the problem:

○ **Overlap each layer slightly.**

○ **Wet the joints and tease the edges together with a pin or soft brush, or pat with the bristles of a toothbrush.**

○ **Hit a joint from either side with a stream of water from a spray bottle. This must be handled deftly and with a delicate touch, or you might damage the casting.**

Framing in Style

There was one perfect frame on clearance for family wedding pictures when three were needed. A solution? Cast paper frames! For uniform cast thickness and best results, make a sheet of cotton linter pulp.

Materials

- Papermaking supplies (*see page 25*)
- 36 cotton linter squares
- Paper additive (calcium carbonate)
- Kitchen butter knife
- Textured metal frame
- Matte sealer (optional)
- Double-stick glue dots or mounting pads
- Photo(s) to mount

Instructions

1. Blend the cotton linter squares with ½ teaspoon of paper additive and 4 cups of water. Pour into a 5½" × 8½" hand mold. For 8½" × 11" deckles, twice as much cotton linter is needed. Repeat blending before forming a sheet.

2. Agitate pulp with fingers to separate fibers. Raise hand mold quickly. Cotton linter clumps (flocks) normally and looks lumpy on the screen. If bare screen can be seen, refloat or reblend and try again.

3. Remove sheet from hand mold. Sponge once over surface to remove water.

4. Use kitchen butter knife to separate sheet into sections sized to lay over sides and top of frame. Pick up sections and place on frame. To bond sections together, overlap where ends meet or pat extra pulp over seams.

5. Use fingers to press cotton linter in frame details. Remove water with sponge, while continuing to work pulp into details.

6. Press and remove as much water as possible. Texture from and details of the design will appear through the back of the cotton linter sheet. A final press with a kitchen towel is a good idea.

7. Tear pulp away from frame edges and center. Set aside to dry.

8. Repeat steps 1 through 7 for additional frames.

9. Optional: Spray a matte sealer over plain or spray-painted casts to offer protection from dust and handling.

Frame Support

Attach frames to matted photographs with glue dots or mounting pads, which work well to attach irregular cast paper to smooth project surfaces. Add dimension by mounting a cast paper frame over a made-to-size cardboard mat covered with recycled or complementary print paper.

O Read up on cotton linter (*see page 125*).

O Do not exceed 36 squares in the blender.

O Recycled pulp will also work for this project, but additives in manufactured paper may cause pulp to stick. Use a release agent (*see page 128*).

Surface Decoration

A pure white, dimensional cast paper surface is beautiful. But you might enjoy experimenting with decorative surface treatments, using a variety of art materials. It's important to note the following factors can influence the clarity of detail in a paper-cast image: tints and additives in cotton linter pulp, the use of recycled fiber, fixatives or sealers applied to the cast before decoration, or the decorations themselves.

Surface Application Ideas

Here is a list of suggested surface decorations to help you get started. First, use a matte or gloss spray sealer to give casts a better surface for decorative finishes.

Chalk or eye shadow. Apply with foam brush, sponge applicators, or synthetic cotton balls. Use a light touch. Use up those old multicolor eye shadow palettes!

Ink pads. Try small, raised ink pads or dual-color pad markers. Lightly brush across raised details of a cast.

Spray paint. Metallic or monochromatic color can be dramatic. Be sure to read warnings on labels and use in a well-ventilated area.

Acrylic paint. It's not good for tinting linter, but it's fine for painting on the surface. It won't feather, even on an untreated paper cast.

Glitter glue. Highlight raised cast details with iridescent or color glitter glues. Also try glitter glue tinted with watercolor, or lightly color the cast with colored pencil and brush diluted glitter glue over the entire cast.

Spray glitter. When a hint of pearlescence or festive sparkle is needed, try using spray glitter. It may be beneficial to use a surface sealant before applying. Again, check all labels and use in a well-ventilated area.

Stuck on You

Attach dry paper casts to another paper surface with any household or craft glue. For best results, use double-stick glue dots or mounting pads, which conform to uneven cast surfaces for better adherence.

Gilding/gold leaf. Follow directions on adhesive designed specifically for gilding applications.

Fine-powdered pigments. Create a lustrous metallic or pearlescent finish. These powders must be mixed with another art medium before application. Mix with acrylic matte or gloss medium to create a paint; mix with acrylic matte or gloss medium and a little bit of water for use in a mouth atomizer for a spray finish; or apply with a blending tool by dipping the applicator directly into the container.

How to Get Colored Pulps

All the color techniques from the previous chapters of this book can certainly be applied to paper casting. And, as stated before, the easiest, least expensive, and fastest way to get colored pulp is by recycling color wastepaper with water in a blender. But feel free to pursue any path to colored pulp that your time, interest level, and talent indicate; that's part of the excitement of the craft and art world.

Casting with Color

In addition to surface decoration or using colored pulp, color can be applied within the cast itself. Some molds' details may provide walls and dividers to help confine colors to selected areas. Different-colored pulps can be put on and in areas with a turkey baster. Push edges into place with a plastic spatula or similar tool. Removing some water will help stabilize it as adjacent pulp colors are placed. After the colors are laid on, layer a wet pulp patty or newly formed sheet of recycled paper or cotton linter over the entire mold. Use a sponge to press and meld the colored pulp decoration to the wet sheet backing. Experience will bring you greater skill with results you never dreamed possible.

Cast Paper Bowls

These elegant bowls are cast with fabric strips that are wrapped around the mold and embedded in the pulp. What a great combination of color and technique!

Materials

- Papermaking supplies (*see page 25*)
- Bowl to use as a mold
- Enough pulp to cover your mold
- Vegetable oil for a release agent (spray or apply with a paper towel)
- Thin strips of torn fabric

Instructions

1. Set up the papermaking screen and support screen over a tray or other container for drainage (*see page 79*).

2. Apply the vegetable oil to the outside of the bowl and set it aside.

3. Prepare the fabric strips by dipping them into pulpy water, and set them aside.

4. Pour pulp onto the screen in a circular shape large enough to cover the outside of the bowl.

5. Place the greased bowl bottom-side down in the center of pulp. Use the papermaking screen to lift the pulp up and onto the mold. Press through the screen with a sponge to shape the pulp against the mold. The pulp will be doubled up and thicker in places where it overlaps, but not to worry. You can even things out as you continue blotting.

6. Turn the bowl bottom side up. Slowly pull up the screen edges and remove it as you work your way around the bowl. Leave the pulp relatively wet for applying fabric.

7. Wrap the fabric around and around the bowl in a spiral. Use the screen and a sponge to press around the bowl, slowly removing as much water as possible. Be careful not to blot too hard, or the pulp might slip on the oily surface. Patch any holes with pieces of wet pulp, and blot again with a sponge. Allow the casting to air dry; if using a glass or ceramic mold, you can dry it in a 150°F oven for an hour or two.

8. When completely dry, release the paper casting from the mold.

Basket Variation

These charming little baskets are made in the same way as the bowls, with just a few differences.

Additional Materials

O The example was made with a stemless wine glass as the mold

O Bits of yarn, feathers, or other embellishments (optional)

O Punched out paper flowers (optional)

O ½"-wide strips of chipboard or scrap cardboard (such as cereal boxes) for handles

O Scrapbooking brads

Instructions

1. Follow the same steps as for the bowl, with one exception. If you want embedded materials, such as the feathers, on the outside of the bowl, lay them on the screen before you pour your pulp. If you want them on the inside, like the yarn in the yellow bowl, press them into the pulp after you pour it and before shaping the pulp onto the mold.

2. When the casting is completely dry and removed from the mold, attach any dry embellishments, such as the flower shapes. Brads work well for this, keeping the attachments secure and three-dimensional.

3. Cut the cardboard strips to the length you like for handles. Use a pencil to mark opposite sides of the basket where you want to attach the handles. Use brads to press holes through the basket and then through each end of the cardboard strip, and bend the ends open to secure.

Tiger Mask

This project is sure to be a hit any time of year. With variations on the ears, this mask can be converted to just about any animal of choice.

Materials

○ Papermaking supplies (*see page 25*), including two papermaking screens (use flexible window screen for good drainage)

○ Enough pulp to cover your mold (orange, white, and black)

○ Plastic face mask with no embellishments, to use as a mold

○ Vegetable oil for a release agent (spray or apply with a paper towel)

○ Round molds, such as tin cans (small, medium, and large, for the eyes and mouth)

○ Tweezers (optional)

○ Six pieces of wire for whiskers

○ Small sharp utility knife or sharp pointed scissors

○ Hole punch

○ Strip of ½" elastic or ribbon, long enough to hold the mask in place

Instructions

1. Set up the papermaking screen and support screen over a tray or other container for drainage.

2. Using orange pulp, pour shapes for the main part of mask and two ears.

3. Place another papermaking screen on top of the pulp and blot with a sponge, but do not flatten completely as you normally would. Leave it a little bit wet, so the pulp is still moldable. Remove the top screen.

4. Coat the outside of the face mask mold with vegetable oil.

5. Use the papermaking screen to lift the orange pulp, turn it over, and place it carefully over the top of the greased mold. Use the second papermaking screen to replace the one you lifted, and set the mask on top of it. Carefully push pulp around with your hands, so that it molds to the shape of the plastic mask, but do not press out all water in the process. Layer the ear shapes on to the sides of the orange base color.

6. Use white pulp to pour white circles — two medium and one large — for the eyes and mouth area. In the same way as the orange pulp, blot and layer the white circles onto the mask mold. Position them carefully and release them from the screen by blotting with a wet sponge.

7. In the same way, use black pulp to pour two small circles for eyes. Blot and layer them onto the mask.

8. Add eyelashes and whisker dots by rolling up pieces of pulp and layering them on to the mask (or use pin-drawing technique, *page 94*). You may want to use tweezers to move the small bits around.

9. On the papermaking screen, form three triangles in black pulp for each side of the mask. Blot, lift, and layer them in place.

10. Using the screen and a sponge, work your way around the mold, pressing and blotting. Don't press too hard, or the paper may slip on the greasy surface.

11. Once the shape seems secure and less wet, allow it to air dry. When completely dry, release it from the mold.

12. Press the wires into the mask for whiskers.

13. Use a utility knife or scissors to cut out eye holes in the black circles.

14. Punch a hole on both sides of the mask, below the ears. Thread the elastic through the holes, adjust for size, and tie the ends on both sides of the mask. Or if using ribbon, attach two strips, one on each side, and tie the ends to fit at the back. Put on the mask and grrrrowl!

Fish Bowl

This project uses the self-bonding technique, so there is no need to press or iron dry the fiber fish. A medium-sized plastic bowl makes the best mold, since it is flexible, though metal or glass bowls also will work. You will need to make 20 to 40 handmade paper fish, depending on the size of the bowl you have chosen. You will be using the *outside* of the bowl as the mold, not the inside. Avoid bowls with prominent rims at the base.

Materials

- Six different-colored 8½" × 11" papers
- Papermaking supplies (*see page 25*)
- Six containers (32 oz. size or greater)
- Bowl: choose an eye-pleasing shape (this bowl was 4" tall with a 10" diameter)
- Clear kitchen plastic wrap
- Fish-shaped cookie cutter
- Cake pan or tray
- Turkey baster
- Paper towels
- Paintbrush (optional)
- Decoupage glue (optional)

Instructions

1. Find wastepaper in six colors you like. For each color of pulp, you will need to recycle an 8½" × 11" sized paper sheet. You can mix and match pieces of similarly hued paper to recycle, but the surface area should roughly add up to this.

2. Tear and blend your first color of pulp in the blender with 4 cups of water. Pour the pulp and all of the water into your first container.

3. Repeat step 2 for the remaining five papers, so you have six colors of pulp in your containers.

4. Place your bowl upside down on your work surface and cover the outside of the bowl with clear kitchen plastic wrap. Try to wrap the bowl smoothly, as the wrinkles in the plastic could show up as texture on the inside of your finished fish bowl. Allow several inches of plastic to hang off the rim to make removal of your finished paper bowl easier.

5. Begin making paper fish by placing a papermaking screen on top of your drain rack in a tray. Place the fish-shaped cookie cutter on top of the screen. Depending on the size of your cookie cutter, you may be able to fit two to three fish on a single screen.

6. Use the turkey baster to suction pulp out of one of your containers and then squirt the pulp into the fish cookie cutter. If the cookie cutter is moving around, use your free hand to hold it in place. Fill the cookie cutter ⅛" deep with pulp.

7. Remove the cookie cutter by pulling straight up. Try not to smear the pulp or decapitate your fish! If there is room on your papermaking screen, create two to three more fish by repeating steps 5 and 6. If you want a contrasting color for the bottom of the bowl, make a circle of pulp to fit.

8. Place the cover screen on top of the fish on the papermaking screen. Use a damp sponge to remove as much water as possible, until the fish peel up easily. Use a paper towel to remove additional water, if necessary.

9. Peel your handmade fish off of the papermaking screen and place the wet paper fish (and the contrasting circle shape, if desired) on the plastic wrap covering the bowl.

10. Repeat steps 6 through 9, overlapping fish and allowing them to point in all directions. Gently press the wet fibers of overlapping fish together with your fingers. Continue until the outside of the bowl is covered with at least two layers of overlapping fish. You can leave several fins or fish lips sticking out along the rim of the bowl for a nice effect. Periodically empty the tray under your draining rack.

11. Let your bowl air dry two to three days (longer in very humid climates), until it is entirely dry. The colors may become less vibrant as the water evaporates from your paper, but as the water is removed, the bonds between your paper bowl's fibers become stronger and stronger.

12. Pull up on the plastic wrap gently to free your fully dried fish bowl. If you used a plastic bowl for a mold, squeeze the sides of your plastic bowl and have a friend help by pulling on the plastic wrap.

13. Optional: Use a paintbrush and decoupage glue to preserve your bowl. Since the bowl is made of paper, if it gets wet, it could turn back into pulp or lose its shape. The glaze protects your bowl over time. Apply one coat and let dry overnight. Apply an additional coat the next day, if desired.

Chapter 8

Making Things with Paper

Once you're hooked on the process of papermaking, you'll no doubt be making sheet after sheet from all kinds of interesting materials. What to do with all that handmade paper? **The possibilities are endless, as you'll find with the beautiful projects presented in this chapter. Give your one-of-a-kind creations as gifts or keep them for personal use as home décor, jewelry, or scrapbooking elements.**

Bookmarks

A bookmark made of paper and words: How appropriate is that? As an added bonus, it clips to your page, so you aren't losing your spot if the pages of your book fall open. The paper shown was made with the mottled surface technique (*see page 62*), using old crossword puzzle pages and tissue paper.

Materials

- O 1¼" x 5" paper strip (per bookmark)
- O Scoring tool (bone folder)
- O Needle and thread
- O ⅛"-wide double-sided tape
- O Large-sized paper clip
- O Several handmade paper scraps
- O Paper punches (we used a small "burst," medium flower, and simple circle)
- O Scissors
- O Hot glue gun and glue sticks or white glue
- O Rubber alphabet stamps and ink pad(s)

Instructions

1. Use the scoring tool to mark lines on a strip of paper, across its long side (or width), approximately ⅛" apart. *Note:* It's important to score handmade paper before folding, because otherwise it may crack or fold poorly.

2. Make accordion folds along the scored lines.

3. Thread a needle, make a knot, and pierce the middle of folded strip. Pull the thread through, tie a knot, and cut the thread.

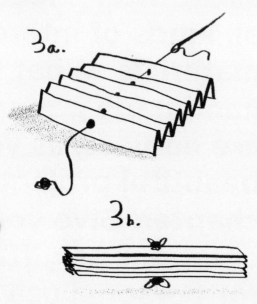

Bone Folder

This handy tool, commonly used in bookbinding, is about the size and shape of a letter opener. In a process called *scoring*, a bone folder is used to make a creased line in paper, to make it easier to fold. Is a bone folder really made of bone? They used to be, and some still are, but they are now more likely to be made of plastic.

4. Open up both ends of the folded stack like a fan. Make a circle by using double-sided tape to attach the folded edges.

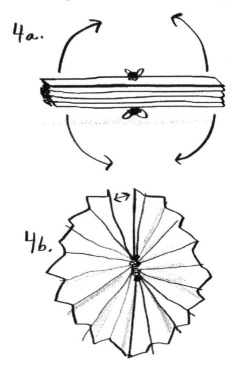

5. Position one end of a paper clip on the back of the pleated circle. Secure it with double-sided tape, covered with a flat paper circle that is a bit smaller than the pleated circle.

6. Use paper punches and scrap paper to create decorative shapes or cut them freehand with scissors.

7. Decorate the front by gluing on punched-out shapes and/or stamping with a word or image.

Mini Circular Cards

These cute little cards make great gift enclosures. The tops were made with flower-punched origami paper embedded on the surface (*see page 64*). The paper attached with ribbon is plain and simple, for writing on. Another idea: Make shaped cards using cookie cutters.

Materials

- Two handmade paper circles (per card), your choice of size
- Standard hole punch
- Scraps of ⅛"-wide ribbon

Instructions

1. Match up two paper circles and use standard hole punch to create hole on the left side through both cards. *Note:* If you're using plain paper circles without embedded decoration, feel free to cut and glue other paper shapes on the top paper circle.

2. Thread the ribbon through both holes, from back to front, and tie the ends together on top.

Paper Circle Sizes

The round papers you'll see in some of these projects are all made with the tin can papermaking technique (*see page 42*). Since the size of the paper circles depends on what you use for your mold, we'll leave that up to you. Average size is from 2¾" to 4". Think of the projects as a jumping-off place for your own creativity. No need to follow instructions to the letter.

Gift wrap and origami paper scraps add a lively decorative touch.

Circular Notes

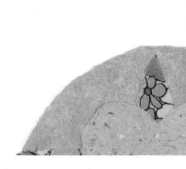

Use round papers with internal or surface embedment (*see pages 64–70*) for these single-circle postcard-style notes. Decorate one side and write (or simply sign your name) on the other. A more advanced project would be to experiment with sheet layering (*see page 110*), which produces paper that is a different color on each side.

Materials

- Round sheets of handmade paper with embedded decorations
- Several handmade paper scraps (optional)
- ⅛"-wide double-sided tape or glue stick (optional)
- Rubber alphabet stamps and ink pad(s)

Crafty Tip

The materials embedded in the notes shown include fabric scraps, bits of string, and pressed bougainvillea petals and clover leaves. Botanicals work great in handmade paper (*see page 66*).

Instructions

1. If you like, cut out shapes from the paper scraps, and add them to the front of the round handmade paper circles. Attach them with double-sided tape or glue stick.

2. Stamp a personal message on the cards, as desired.

3. Optional: Make your own envelopes (*see page 189*).

Paper Cones

These little cones are handy for party favors, just the right size to fill with jelly beans or other candy favorites. Since you need square paper, you can either cut a longer sheet to size or custom-make square paper, using an old square picture frame as a mold. For the pulp, we used colored napkins, an old paper bag, and a paper towel.

Materials

- 5½" square of handmade paper (per cone)
- Scissors
- Clear tape
- Pencil or pen
- Hole punch
- 8" colored string, ribbon, or yarn
- Rubber stamps and ink pad(s) or label maker (optional)

Instructions

1. Trim off the rough edges on two sides of the paper square using scissors; these should be adjacent sides, not opposite one another. If you want the top edge of the cone to be smooth, as shown in the project, trim all four edges.

2. Practice rolling the cone by bringing the two adjacent trimmed sides of the paper together. Unroll the cone and lay a piece of tape along one inside cut edge with half of the tape hanging off the edge (the second cut edge will be attached there).

3. Roll the cone back into shape, carefully pressing the cut edges together and matching up the tip and base of cone. To ensure a strong joint, use the back of pencil, pen, or fingernail to smooth the tape down securely.

4. Punch a hole in the top corner of the cone. The hole should be large enough to accommodate whatever ribbon or string you decide to use as your hanging loop.

5. Tie the 8" piece of string into a loop, with a knot larger than the punched hole. Pull the looped end through the hole; the knot should keep it from passing through.

6. Optional: Add labels to the front of the cones, depending on intended use.

Crafty Tips

- To save time, reuse/recycle the pulp colors. Use the base color from a cone for the decorative colors on another cone.

- Blend the pulp to a very smooth consistency for pulp gun painting. Use a pastry icing squeeze bottle or an old honey bottle. The tip should be at least ³⁄₁₆" in diameter or pulp will clog and come out in uneven spurts.

- Blend pulp very smoothly for the square cone paper. Mottled materials don't curve/bend very well.

Tin Can Critters

Use whatever mottled-surface paper you like for these sweet little critters. Paint on the details (black-and-white eyes, pink ears, orange beak, black dots) with pulp as you make the paper (*see page 84*). If you prefer, punch circles from paper instead and glue them on after making each critter, then make eye centers with a felt marker.

Fish

The fish can be made entirely with pulp layering (*see page 78*). Just for fun, embed opalescent confetti into the pulp when making the paper.

1. Start with a large circle of pulp, and layer on heart-shaped pulp for the tail.

2. Add a circle of white pulp for the eye and black for the pupil.

Mouse

Materials

- One large paper circle for the body and two for the ears
- ⅛"-wide double-sided tape
- Yarn scrap for the tail

Instructions

1. Fold the larger body circle in half to create a two-layer semicircle.

2. Attach one ear on each layer using double-sided tape.

3. Tuck one end of the yarn tail inside the folded body and attach with double-sided tape.

Bird

Materials

- o 10" bamboo skewer for legs, or two toothpicks for short legs
- o Utility knife
- o One paper circle for the body, or two for double-sided bird
- o Clear tape
- o ⅛"-wide double-sided tape
- o Bits of feathers
- o Glue stick or white glue

Instructions

1. Trim off one sharp end of each skewer with a utility knife to avoid poking holes in the body paper. Position the blunt ends on the back of the paper and attach with tape.

2. Optional: If making a double-sided bird, attach the second circle to the back of bird using double-sided tape, sandwiching the leg sticks between the two layers.

3. Glue on bits of feathers as you like.

Ladybug

Materials

- o One red paper circle for the wings
- o One black paper circle slightly larger than the red circle
- o ⅛"-wide double-sided tape
- o Black felt-tipped marker (optional)

Instructions

1. Cut the red circle down the middle, but leave it attached at one end.

2. Cut the black circle into a teardrop shape.

3. Attach the red ladybug wings circle on top of the black teardrop body with double-sided tape.

Cupcake Toppers

These cheerful shapes were made using a handmade pie-tin mold for the bird (*see page 81*) and cookie cutter molds for the flowers (*see page 80*). The decorations on the flowers were made from origami paper, wrapping paper, napkins, and construction paper embedded in the surface as the paper was made (*see page 64*).

Materials

- Hole punch
- Handmade paper bird and flower shapes (two per double-sided topper)
- 10" bamboo skewers (one per flower; two per bird)
- Clear tape
- Pencil
- ⅛"-wide double-sided tape

Bird

1. Punch a hole for bird's eye.

2. Affix two skewers to the back of bird body shape with clear tape. Rub down with a pencil or fingernail to ensure a secure joint.

3. Hide the taped skewer tops in a double-sided bird by attaching a second bird shape on the back of the other with double-sided tape.

Flowers

1. Affix a skewer to the back the paper flower shape with clear tape. Rub down with a pencil or fingernail to ensure a secure joint.

2. Hide the taped skewer top in a double-sided flower by attaching a second flower shape on the back of the other with double-sided tape.

Flowers

Create a floral display anytime of the year with these fun-and-easy flowers. The large background paper circles were made with embedded bougainvillea petals (*see page 66*), and the inside flower shapes and leaves were made with shaped cookie cutter molds. Centers were made using a pulp gun (*see page 27*).

Materials

- O 10" square of newspaper
- O 1/8"-wide clear or double-sided tape
- O Scissors
- O Cardboard
- O One large paper circle with embedded petals and one smaller molded or cut-out flower shape per flower (two each for double-sided flowers)
- O Two to four leaf shapes per flower

Instructions

1. Roll a section of newspaper on the diagonal into a tight tube to make the flower stem. Tape the end with clear tape or use double-sided tape if you don't want the tape to show.

2. Cut a 1/4" cardboard square and attach it to the back of a small flower shape with double-sided tape. This is to give the flower a bit of dimension. *Note:* If your flower shapes are tiny, the 1/4" cardboard square may be too big; cut to a size that will ensure you don't see cardboard peeking out from behind the flower shape.

3. Tape the flower shape to the embedded-petal circle and then tape the circle to the front of the stem. For double-sided flowers, repeat steps 2 and 3, matching the second circle to the first on the opposite side of the stem and taping the two together with double-sided tape.

4. Lay two leaves together at the points and tape them together on the back. Tape the pair to the stem as desired. For double-sided flowers, repeat this step on opposite side of stem and secure leaf sets to one another with double-sided tape.

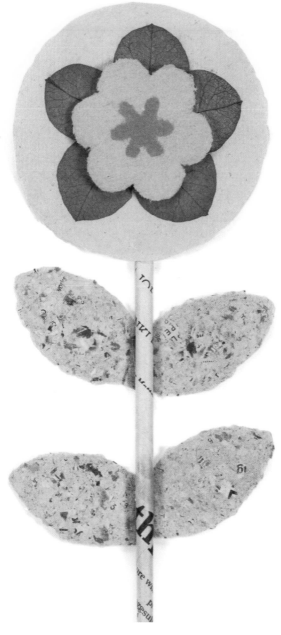

Simple Mini Name Garland

This simple garland can be hung on a door or wall, but is just as cute as a personal touch to gift wrapping. Instead of just plain ribbon around a package, create this mini garland with recipient's name. It uses a variety of shapes, made with pulp poured into cookie cutters and aspic cutters (*see page 80*). When making the paper, add extra water to the pulp and use a squeeze bottle with a small nozzle, to make pouring into small molds easier.

Materials

O Several paper shapes in varying sizes (we used flowers, circles, hearts and teardrops)

O Rubber alphabet stamps and ink pad(s)

O Strip of ½"-wide ribbon

O ⅛"-wide double-sided tape

Instructions

1. Decorate the shapes with stamps, as desired.

2. Lay the ribbon out on the table.

3. Put a small piece of double-sided tape on the back of each shape and affix them to the ribbon. Rub hard on back of ribbon to make sure shape and ribbon are joined securely.

4. Tie loops at both ends of the ribbon for hanging.

Name Garland

Name personalization is a popular trend in decorating kids' rooms, but retail lettered wall hangings can be pricey. Create the same personal flair in your child's room with this adorable name garland, without the expense. The letters on these circles are made with the pulp painting technique (*see page 84*). We used very smoothly pureed pulp, in two contrasting colors.

Materials

- ⅛"-wide double-sided tape
- Paper circles that spell out a name
- ½"-wide ribbon or bias tape (the length will depend on the desired length of the finished project)

Instructions

1. Attach piece of double-sided tape across the center back of each circle.

2. Create a loop on one end of the ribbon or bias tape, using double-sided tape to adhere ribbon end to ribbon.

3. Affix ribbon to back of first letter and work your way over to the last letter, pressing the ribbon firmly to the tape as you go.

4. Finish the garland with another closed loop for hanging.

Deluxe Garland

The circles for this garland were made with the mottled surface technique (*see page 62*). Pulp made from old tissue paper, paper napkins, and old wrapping paper was poured into cookie cutter and tin-can molds (*see page 80*). Some decorative elements were added with pulp layering (*see page 78*). The instructions that follow are for a one-sided garland about 3 feet in length.

Materials

○ Twelve 4"-diameter shapes (we used circles and flowers)

○ ⅛"-wide double-sided tape

○ Ruler or measuring tape

○ Approximately 6 feet string, ribbon, bias tape, or fabric

Instructions

1. Plan out the order of the shapes and lay them out on a long table. Carefully turn over each shape, keeping them in the correct position.

2. Cut 4" strips of double-sided tape (the width of each shape) and affix them down the center backs of the shapes.

3. Lay out the ribbon or other connecting strips on the table. Fold it in half to make two long strands. The top folded end will become the top loop for hanging. Affix the ribbon to the back of each shape, one at a time. Spaces can be left between the shapes, or shapes can be butted up next to each other.

Crafty Tips

○ To save time, prepare four flowers at once.

○ Instead of three layers of paper on each shape, simplify to two layers.

○ Remember to rinse the molds you are reusing each time you change colors.

○ When using certain colored papers, color may run onto the paper towel (used for blotting) and may transfer onto other colors if the paper towel is reused.

○ Pour the base (first) color a little heavier than subsequent layers, to ensure sturdiness.

○ When using smaller molds, mix a little more water into the pulp for ease of pouring.

○ Hot glue gun can be used for a more secure attachment, if required, instead of double-sided tape.

Gift Wrap Embellishment and Tags

Just as with the Simple Mini Name Garland (*see page 158*), this project dresses up typical gift wrapping. It's also a good project for using up scraps from other projects; use circular paper or cut or punch circles from scraps.

Materials

- O Small and medium paper punches
- O 1" handmade paper circles (10 shapes per 1' length)
- O String
- O Clear tape
- O Glue stick or white glue
- O 2½" to 3" handmade paper circle

Instructions

1. Use paper punches to make interesting shapes inside the 1" paper circles. Set aside paper punch-outs for use in decorating the tag, step 4.

2. Lay out the paper circles in desired order, with about ¼" between them.

3. Attach string to the back side of the circles using clear tape.

4. Glue paper punch-outs from step 1 to the large paper circle to make the coordinating gift tag.

Decorate one side of the tag and keep the other side blank for a personal message.

Holiday Wreath

This charming wreath can be made in colors to match any season: red and brown for autumn, red and green for the holidays, or pastels for spring. The sample shown here was created primarily with mottled paper, made from a brown paper bag, gold origami paper, and a paper-lined candy wrapper, with glitter thrown in. Most shapes were molded in shaped cookie cutters, with the oak leaves cast in a custom-shaped pie tin (*see page 81*) and embedded with pieces of metallic string.

Materials

- Pencil or pen
- 8"-diameter mixing bowl
- 8½" square cardboard
- 7"-diameter mixing bowl
- One paper clip or equivalent length of wire
- 1"-wide masking tape
- 18 red handmade paper circles
- 18 white handmade paper circles
- Stapler and staples
- 11 brown leaves
- Four brown oak leaves (optional)

Instructions

1. Place the 8" mixing bowl onto the cardboard, trace around it, and cut out the circle.

2. Center the 7" bowl inside the cut circle, trace, and cut out to make the ring backing for the wreath.

3. Bend the wire or paper clip into a loop with two tails and attach the loop to the back of cardboard with masking tape, as shown, to create the wreath hanger.

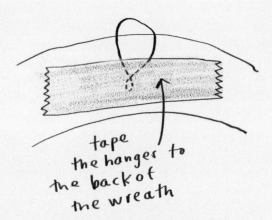

tape the hanger to the back of the wreath

4. Position the white and red circles around the cardboard ring to plan placement. Staple them in place, one at a time, to the cardboard ring, curling the shapes at one end to give them a bit of volume. Overlap each row of red and white circles as you go around the ring to hide the staples in the previous row.

5. Staple the simple leaf shapes on top of the circles in the same way.

6. Optional: Tape the oak leaves to the back of the cardboard ring or tuck them behind other leaves and staple them in place.

Illustrated Cards

Here's a great project for letting your imagination go wild. It's also a good way to use up scraps from other projects. You can custom-make shapes to fit the scene you have in mind for your card.

Materials

- Ruler
- 8½" × 11" sheet of thick handmade paper or commercial cardstock
- Scissors or utility knife
- Scoring tool (bone folder)
- Handmade paper scraps
- Glue stick

Instructions

1. Measure the halfway point of the 11" side of the paper/cardstock sheets and cut them in half to make 5½" × 8½" sheets.

2. Measure and score each paper/cardstock piece to make two cards that will be 5½" × 4¼" when folded.

3. Plan your design. You can make templates to use for cutting out the pieces from the handmade paper scraps, or cut them out freehand.

4. Lay out your design on the card. When you're satisfied with the arrangement, secure the pieces with glue stick.

Mailing Your Cards

These instructions are for cards that will fit a standard envelope size. To make your own custom envelopes, see the suggestions on page 189.

Jar Lid Labels

What a great way to personalize your homemade creations! Use the tin-can papermaking method (*see page 42*), with a mold that is at least ¼" larger than the lid you want to cover. These were made by adding cut-out shapes, ribbon, and rickrack to the pulp, using the surface embedment technique (*see page 64*).

Materials

- Handmade paper circle (slightly larger than jar lid)
- Glue stick
- Canning jars and lids
- Utility knife

Instructions

1. Lay the handmade paper circle face down on a flat, protected surface and coat with glue stick.

2. Center the jar lid, top down, on the paper. Turn over both lid and paper and use your finger to smooth the paper over the lid. Press firmly.

3. Trim the excess paper from around the circle, using a utility knife.

Other Label Ideas

Some of these labels were cut from handmade paper, and some were made to fit, using cookie cutter shapes. If you are making paper to fit, measure the label surface and keep in mind that paper tends to "grow" an unknown amount when it's flattened and dried. You can embed white paper in the surface as you make the labels (*see page 64*), or glue on white paper shapes after the paper is dry. Finished labels can be attached to most any surface using glue stick.

Magnets

The paper for these little cuties was made with aspic molds and the pulp layering technique (*see page 78*). You can also custom-shape your own molds from aluminum pie tins (*see page 81*).

Materials

- O Rubber stamps and ink pad(s) (optional)
- O Handmade paper circles
- O Heavy-duty double-sided tape or craft glue
- O 1″ or smaller magnetic disks

Instructions

1. Use rubber stamps to decorate the paper circles, if desired, and then flip the circles face down.

2. Press squares of double-sided tape or place a dot of glue on the back of each magnet.

3. Center the glue side of the magnets on the back of each paper circle and press hard to attach.

Simple Mobile

This project has a lovely result without a great deal of effort. Use paper that is thick enough to be sturdy, but thin enough to fit in the paper punch. The paper shown here was made with phone book pages and wrapping paper. The pretty colors came from recycled tissue paper and party napkins that were crumpled and no longer fit for entertaining.

Materials

- O 1½" flower-shaped paper punch
- O Eight circles of paper, at least 3" in diameter
- O ¹⁄₁₆"-hole paper punch
- O Scissors
- O Colored cotton string or topstitching thread
- O 12" stick

Instructions

1. Punch out flower shapes in the center of each handmade paper circle.

2. Lay out the circles and the flower shapes in three rows, alternating the shapes as shown in the project photo.

3. Use the hole punch to make small holes in the top of each paper piece, for attaching the string.

4. Cut 1¼" pieces of string and run them through the holes one at a time. Tie off with knots.

5. Position the stick horizontally at the top and tie on all three embellished strings. Since the papers are all about the same size and weight, the mobile should balance.

6. Tie another string at the top, with a knot at each end, and long enough to make a loop for hanging.

Mobile Imagination

Find an interesting rod or stick, and use simple shapes to make up your own design. Keep experimenting until you find the right balance.

Cloud Mobile

This mobile is a sweet addition to the wall décor of a baby's room. The pulp for these papers was made with gift wrap, newspaper, and construction paper. The cloud was assembled and pressed all as one piece, using the pulp layering technique (*see page 78*), but you can glue individual dried paper circles together. The raindrops were made with homemade pie tin molds in three different sizes.

Materials

- Pulp-layered cloud shape (or an assortment of 3" and 4" circles taped or glued together)
- Scissors
- 80" colored cotton string or topstitching thread
- 12 paper raindrops in varying sizes
- Needle and thread or $\frac{1}{16}$" hole punch
- Short length of flexible wire (optional), if hanging on the wall
- Clear tape

Instructions

1. Begin with an evenly balanced cloud shape, whether pulp-layered or created from individual circles that are over-lapped and taped or glued together into a cloud shape.

2. Cut three pieces string or thread, each 24" long.

3. Lay out the raindrops on a flat surface in varying positions along the three strings.

4. Use a needle and thread or a hole punch to make holes in the top of each rain-drop, as well as three holes equally spaced on the bottom of the cloud shape.

5. Knot string/thread to keep each rain-drop in place.

6. Attach a string to the top of mobile, with one end on each side and enough to make a loop for hanging. (Another option is to attach a wire loop to the back, if the mobile will be hung against a wall.)

7. Test the balance of the mobile by temporarily taping the three raindrop-embellished strings to the back of the cloud and then hanging the mobile. Adjust the position of the strings as necessary. When satisfied, permanently attach strings to the cloud by creating three holes with hole punch or needle and knotting the raindrop strings in place.

Shelf Edging

This shelf edging is adorable in a child's bedroom or perhaps on a small kitchen shelf full of cookbooks. The circles were made using the surface embedment technique (*see page 64*), with very thin fabrics made of natural fibers.

Materials

- O Three 4"-diameter handmade paper circles for every foot of shelf edging
- O Ruler
- O Utility knife
- O 1"-wide double-fold bias tape
- O ¼"-wide fusible tape
- O Press cloth
- O Iron

Instructions

1. Cut handmade paper circles in half down the middle, using a ruler and sharp utility knife. Be sure circles are completely dry before cutting.

2. Open up the bias tape, lay a strip of fusible tape across the bottom edge, arrange the half-circles side-by-side with the tape underneath. Place another strip of fusible tape on top of the circles, and fold down the top edge of bias tape (with the circle edges and tape sandwiched within).

3. Place press cloth over sandwiched edging and press with a hot iron to adhere all layers together.

Crafty Tips

- O Circles can be smaller or larger or spaced out differently, depending on the desired effect.

- O The banding can be narrower or wider, if preferred. If you can do some basic sewing, you can make your own double-fold bias tape, with a center fold and the edges pressed under. When planning the length, remember to leave enough on each end to tuck them under neatly.

- O You also can use a sewing machine to secure the circles to the fabric, instead of the iron-together method, but some tape will be needed to hold everything together for sewing.

Pencil Wrap

The paper for the center wrap was made with cut-up crossword puzzles, embedded in pureed newsprint (*see page 64*). The pulp was poured a bit on the thin side to help with molding and shaping of the paper.

Materials

- Flexible measuring tape
- Several pencils
- 1¼" × 5½" strips of handmade paper
- Scissors
- ⅛"-wide double-sided tape
- Utility knife

Instructions

1. Measure the circumference and height of the pencils you will be covering. A standard pencil requires about 1¼" × 5½". Trim paper strips to fit.

2. Cover the back of the paper with double-sided tape; two tape strips will usually do it. (Use tape instead of a glue stick for better adhesion.)

3. Press the pencil down along one edge of the paper, keeping the pencil and paper aligned. Tightly roll the rest of the paper around the pencil, pressing against the table surface to help it stick.

4. Trim off any excess paper, as needed, with a utility knife.

Easy Holiday Ornaments

Here are two very easy ornaments to make for your own home during the holidays. They make great gifts for others, too! The star shapes are made with cookie cutter molds (*see page 80*).

Star

Materials

- ○ Scoring tool (bone folder)
- ○ Two handmade paper stars per ornament
- ○ White glue
- ○ Heavy books or weights
- ○ Small hole punch
- ○ 3½" length of 21-gauge beading or craft wire per ornament

Instructions

1. Score both stars down the middle (from the top point to the bottom indent) and fold.

2. Glue them together at the folds, outer fold to outer fold. Lay them flat and weigh down as needed to hold them together while they dry.

3. Punch a hole through both layers at the top of the star.

4. Thread wire through the hole and twist the ends together to make a loop for hanging.

Circles

Materials

- ○ One molded paper circle shape per ornament (the example has embedded foil shapes)
- ○ Paper punches (various sizes and shapes)
- ○ Small hole punch
- ○ 3½" length of 21-gauge beading or craft wire per ornament

Instructions

1. Use paper punches as desired to embellish each molded paper circle, punching around the embedded foil shapes, if applicable.

2. Punch a small hole at the top of the paper circle.

3. Thread wire through the hole and twist the ends together to make a loop for hanging.

Tree Ornament

This ornament makes for an interesting three-dimensional handmade paper addition to your cherished family heirlooms. The pulp for this project sample was made with a brown shopping bag, paper towel, cream construction paper, and glitter (*see page 76*). The mottled look is great, but the more mottled a paper is, the harder it is to curve and bend. To compensate, the pulp was blended until very smooth.

Materials

- Scoring tool (bone folder)
- One 3", 4", and 5" handmade paper circle per ornament
- Scissors or utility knife
- Clear tape
- Colored cotton string or topstitching thread
- White glue (optional)
- Two brown ½" × 3" handmade paper strips per ornament

Instructions

1. Score each circle down the middle, fold in half, and cut along the fold.

2. Roll each half-circle into a cone shape, joining the cut edges on the inside with clear tape. Make sure the tape comes as close to the point as possible.

3. Take 10" piece of string or thread and knot one end, leaving at least a 2" tail (for attaching the trunk later). Thread unknotted end through largest cone, from the inside out through the tip.

4. Tie a new knot 1" up from the top of the large cone and thread through the medium-sized cone.

5. Tie another knot 1" up from the top of the medium cone and thread through the tip of the small cone.

6. Tie a loop at the top for hanging.

7. Place small dots of glue on the knots for reinforcement, if needed.

8. Take the two strips of brown paper and glue them together, sandwiching the 2" tail at the bottom of the ornament between them. Make sure that plenty of the trunk is visible at the bottom of the tree.

Name-on-a-String Cards

Throwing a party? Make custom name cards for your guests with this surface embedment idea!

Materials

- Colored yarn, string, or very thin strips of fabric
- Papermaking supplies (*see page 25*)
- 4" × 6" mold (for instance: a picture frame with the glass and backing removed)
- Scoring tool (bone folder)

Instructions

1. Wet the yarn and test-write the desired names to ensure each strip is long enough.

2. Prepare the pulp and make a sheet of paper (*see page 52*). Remove the mold, but do not press out any water yet.

3. Dip the yarn into pulpy water to coat it with paper fibers. Working on one half of the paper sheet (to allow for folding later), apply the yarn to the poured pulp. Make sure to press it in, so it adheres to the pulp.

4. Process and press the paper as usual.

5. When the paper is dry, score it along the center line, where you plan to fold it; otherwise the paper may crack and fold unevenly (*see* Bone Folder, *page 148*). The folded finished card size will be 3" × 4".

Pose-able Puppet

Fun to make and even more fun to play with, this little puppet could brighten many a rainy day!

Materials

- Variety of handmade paper scraps, including a circular piece for the head
- Yarn or string scraps as desired, for hair or other details
- Small scrapbooking brads for the joints
- Bamboo skewer or wooden craft stick
- Masking or fabric tape

Instructions

1. Make up a pattern for the puppet and use it to cut out the body parts, or cut out the parts freehand. Arrange the pieces together as you like.

2. Using a brad for each joint, attach the head, arms, and legs to the torso. Then attach the hands and feet.

3. Attach the skewer to the back of the torso with tape. Depending on the size of the puppet, you might need two or three pieces of masking or fabric tape to secure.

Custom Notebook or Journal

Try this method when kids want a quick, personal project to make with recycled paper. There are at least two ways the journal can be bound, and you might think up new ways!

Method 1

Materials

- O Scoring tool (bone folder)
- O Thick handmade paper for cover, 5½" × 8"
- O Several sheets handmade paper for interior pages, same size
- O Binding material (cord, string, yarn, ribbon, raffia)

Instructions

1. Score a thick handmade paper sheet down the center and fold it in half to create a book cover.

2. Fold thinner same-sized papers for inside pages. Tuck them inside the folded cover.

3. Open the pages and wrap binding material around the spine of the book to hold the pages in place. Tie the binding material on the outside.

Method 2

Materials

- O Scoring tool (bone folder)
- O Thick handmade paper for cover (*see* Tips)
- O Several sheets handmade paper for interior pages (*see* Tips)
- O Yarn or string
- O Large-eye needle big enough to thread the yarn

Instructions

1. Score a thick handmade paper sheet down the center and fold it in half, or select two sheets for the front and back covers.

2. Select a stack of thinner same-sized papers for the inside pages, and line them up between the cover sheets.

3. Use a pencil to mark stitch holes, evenly spaced along the left edge of the cover.

4. Thread the large-eye needle with yarn, and use the diagram as a guide for the blanket stitch. Be sure to pierce through the front cover, all pages, and the back cover with each stitch.

Crafty Tips

Add longer life to recycled paper pieces by following these tips:

- O Add acid-free additive (calcium carbonate) to pulp to neutralize acid in paper. Acid in paper tends to cause yellowing.
- O Use spray sealer with UV protection or a frame under UV filtering glass.
- O Display out of direct sunlight.

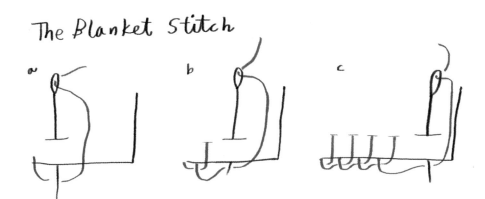

The Blanket Stitch

a   b   c

Tips

- The personal decorations and text were added as the paper was being made, using the surface embedment technique (*see page 64*). The patterned letters were made from the paper inside security envelopes.

- The size of the notebook is up to you. It can be bound with one large cover sheet folded in half, or with two separate sheets for the front and the back. With the second option, you can use larger sheets of paper to produce a larger notebook.

- The example uses a total of 16 interior sheets. More sheets can be used, but if the stack becomes too thick, you may need a hole punch to pierce holes for the binding.

Birthstone Card

Use the surface embedment technique (*see page 64*) to personalize a birthday card, with the name of the month and the birthstone. Or mount the paper on a heavier board with a small loop for hanging on the wall. Paper made from a shopping bag provides a nice backdrop for embedded foil origami paper. (Tin foil doesn't work for embedment, because it contains no paper fiber and will not adhere properly.)

Materials

O Papermaking supplies (*see page 25*)

O Foil origami paper and other colorful patterned paper scraps

Instructions

1. Plan your image in pencil, and cut out paper letters and shapes as desired. You might want to lay them out as a trial run to make sure everything will fit.

2. Prepare recycled paper using your mold of choice (rectangle, square, or circular). While the pulp is still very wet, lightly dip each piece of your design in pulpy water to coat them with fibers, and then press them into the paper.

3. Blot and dry the paper as usual.

Torrent Lampshade

It helps to sketch out your design and to use white or very light-colored sheets of recycled paper to make the lampshade more luminous. Make six to eight different-colored sheets of recycled paper in the usual way. Include at least two light colors. Hold finished papers up to lamp light to see which will look the best on your lampshade.

Materials

- Several sheets handmade paper in assorted colors
- Peel-and-stick adhesive lampshade
- Lit lamp
- Glue stick

The Torrent should be constructed on lampshades that come with peel-and-stick adhesive on styrene liners for fire safety (*see* Resources, *page 196*).

Instructions

1. Tear thin, long strips from various sheets of handmade paper. Because of the curvature of the lampshade, strips will slant diagonally, instead of running straight across.

2. Remove film over adhesive on the lampshade. Place strips on the adhesive, lining up curves and keeping the colors varied.

3. Cover the entire lampshade with torn strips, holding it up to a lit lamp to look for cracks between strips. Disperse light-colored strips throughout for a luminous effect. Tear smaller strips and use your glue stick where multiple pieces overlap.

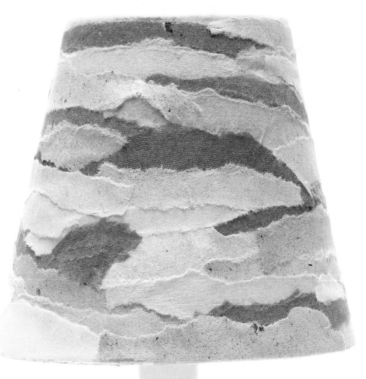

Coiled Bowl

The coiled bowl is a popular project in green magazines and the handmade paper version is a lovely variation. This bowl uses 30 sheets of 5½" × 8½" paper made from recycled wrapping paper, library newsletters, security envelopes, receipts, magazine pages, and tissue paper. The basic steps are papermaking, cutting, folding, and gluing.

Materials

- Papermaking supplies (*see page 25*)
- Scissors
- Large spoon or bone folding tool
- Low-temperature hot glue gun and glue sticks
- Paintbrush (optional)
- Decoupage glue (optional)

Instructions

1. Make 30 sheets of 5½" × 8½" paper in the usual way. The papers for this bowl were ironed dry, though they could be pressed dry.

2. Cut each paper in half lengthwise to make 60 pieces (2¾" × 8½").

3. Take your first piece of handmade paper and fold it in half lengthwise, using a spoon or bone folding tool to make a nice straight edge. Then fold the strip in half (lengthwise) again. Fold in half lengthwise a third time, using the spoon to press the newly folded edge, until the strip is approximately ½" × 8½".

4. Repeat step 3 for the remaining 59 pieces of 2¾" × 8½" papers.

5. Lay folded strips out on work surface in the order you want to use them. Have the fold open to the table (if it were an alligator mouth, it would be trying to eat your table); this is how the strips will be glued into the bowl, with the single fold up and the opening of the fold down. Vary the colored strips in a way that is interesting, and save two of the nicest looking strips for last, as they make the outer rim of the bowl and will be prominently displayed. *Note:* The first two strips are the hardest to coil.

6. Use a low-temperature hot glue gun to put a 1" line of hot glue on the left edge of the first strip (put the line of glue in the middle of the strip).

7. Coil the strip onto the glue, trying not to get your fingers in the hot glue. Also, try to keep the coil straight, so it will sit flat on a table.

8. Continue gluing and coiling in this way until the first strip is completely rolled.

9. Coil the second strip the same way, laying its left edge flush with the end of the first coiled strip. The paper strips in your bowl should not overlap; rather, begin smoothly where the previous strip ended, making a continuously smooth circle. As your coil grows larger, you should be able to put a line of glue much longer than 1".

10. Beginning with the third strip of paper, place a line of hot glue on the outside of the coil, instead of on the inside of the paper strip you are attaching. Wrap the paper strip around the glue and try to

keep your coil level and round. Keep in mind that you don't need to use excessive hot glue, as you don't want beads of glue to stick out in your finished project. Remember, the subsequent coiled strips will hug and hold these strips in place.

11. Repeat step 10 until you have coiled about a third of your total strips (20 strips) into a colorful roll. This will be the base of your bowl, the part that sits flat on the table and holds things like keys, cards, or candies.

12. Begin building up the sides of your bowl by positioning and gluing the next folded paper strip (and each subsequent strip) so the single top-folded edge is slightly (about 2 mm) above the one before it. Continue to line up the left and right edges of strips and gradually build the sides. This very slight rise seems tedious, but will give your bowl a lovely shape. *Note:* To make a taller, narrower bowl, simply increase the rise from your previous strip to ¼" or more.

13. Continue to glue, coil, and build up the sides of your bowl in this way until the last two strips. Use a bit more hot glue on the last two strips to secure them firmly to the bowl. Pay special attention to adding more glue to the right edge of the last folded paper strip, as nothing will come after it.

14. Optional: Use a paintbrush to apply decoupage glue to the inside and outside of your coiled bowl to protect it. Let dry and enjoy!

Pop-Up Cards

Pop-up cards deliver a surprise along with their message. Tin can paper (*see page 42*) carries springy enthusiasm. Handmade glitter sheets (*see page 76*) unfold with joyful holiday greetings. To make your envelopes, see page 189.

Spiral

Materials

- Scissors
- Handmade paper circles
- Blank greeting cards or folded recycled paper (the size is up to you)
- Rubber stamps and ink pad(s) or markers
- Glue stick

Instructions

1. Cut paper circles into a spiral by starting at the outside of each circle and working toward the center.

2. Draw or stamp on the greeting card.

3. Put the spiral face down on the work surface. Cover only the *outside* (largest) ring of the spiral with glue.

4. Press the spiral onto the right inside panel of the card, so the "tail" is closest to the card's center fold.

5. Cover the "head" of the spiral with glue.

6. Close the greeting card and press. The spiral will automatically attach itself in the correct spot to pop up when the card is opened.

Sphere

Materials

- 5½" × 8½" sheet of handmade paper
- Cutting mat
- Tin can
- Pencil
- Template on page 199
- Ruler
- Utility knife
- 1 blank sheet of paper, 1" or so larger than the handmade paper (optional)
- Glue stick

Instructions

1. Fold the finished handmade paper in half to create a guide line. Unfold and place the paper face down on cutting mat.

2. Center a tin can over the fold guide line and trace around the can with a pencil.

3. Using the template as a guide, draw an even number of straight lines with a ruler. With a utility knife, cut along the *lines only*. Cut exactly to the circle's edge for automatic pop-up action.

4. Refold the paper so every other strip of the design folds inward (away from the card's folded edge). If you like, you can stop here, and display the card as a stand-up piece, as shown in the photograph. If you want to make a folded card with a message on the front, continue with the following steps to add another sheet of paper to the outside.

5. Place the folded cut paper on a work surface with the folded edge on the right and the back facing up. Use the glue stick to cover the paper sheet back with adhesive.

6. Fold the blank sheet of paper in half, then open it up. Place the glued paper over the open paper, aligning center folds. Press the glued half into place.

7. Turn the inside sheet to expose the unglued back side. Cover it with adhesive, as before. Close the outer sheet onto the handmade sheet, and press the card onto the adhesive. Place the folded cards under a stack of books until the glue sets.

8. Decorate the outside of the card as you like.

Custom Wedding Invitations

It's not just about economics, the environment, or a certain interest in creative expression. Handmade paper invitations are personal, in a way that commercial invitations can't be. Use any papermaking technique you like best, and keep in mind that if you are doing a lot of invitations, you might want to keep it simple!

Materials

O Handmade paper for the backing (*see* Tip)

O Printouts of the wedding information (*see* Tip)

Fastening options

O Hole punch and ribbon or string

O Needle and thread

O Scrapbooking brad

Instructions

1. Center the printout on top of the handmade paper, and attach the two pages using one of the following methods:

O To attach with ribbon, find the center point along the top edge of the printout where you want the ribbon to be. Punch two holes, one on either side of that center point, through both layers of paper. Thread the ends of a ribbon from the back through the holes and tie them into a bow in front. Once you know how long the ribbon needs to be, you can precut the pieces for the remaining invitations.

O Stitch the top edge of the printout to the back paper using a needle and thread. You might want to design the front papers to print with tiny stitch hole markings that can be used as a guide during assembly.

O Use a scrapbooking brad to pierce the top layer, then the bottom layer, and open up the brad ends to secure.

Together with their parents

Caskey McFerrin

and

Pela Hadley

request the pleasure of your company
at their marriage

SUNDAY, THE THIRD OF SEPTEMBER
AT FIVE-THIRTY IN THE AFTERNOON
MARTHA CLARA VINEYARDS
DINNER RECEPTION TO FOLLOW

Tip

The paper size is up to you, but we recommend handmade paper that is 5½" × 8½", for several reasons:

O This size will fit nicely into a standard 6" × 9" envelope without any need to fold the paper. If you prefer a fold, there are other standard envelopes that will work; just be sure to score the handmade paper before folding (*see* Bone Folder, *page 148*). Of course, you can make your own envelopes, but when planning a wedding, will you have the time?

O The wedding information can be printed efficiently, two side-by-side on a 8½" × 11" paper. When planning the text, be sure to allow a generous margin on the top and sides, as you will need to trim about an inch off all sides to be able to see the handmade paper behind it.

Planning for Success

Things to keep in mind when planning recycled paper wedding invitations:

O It takes time to make paper and assemble invitations. Plan ahead.

O Look through bridal and card-making magazines for invitation ideas. Many popular styles and layouts are easily adapted to paper you make yourself.

O Keep designs simple. A simple torn edge can be beautiful. Stick to one sheet of handmade paper (or less) per invitation set.

O Make a "paper recipe." No two sheets will turn out exactly the same, but a recipe will simplify production.

O Choose a wastepaper base fiber that's easy to come by. Junk mail envelopes are ubiquitous and recycle into quality pulp.

O Add-ins can incorporate wedding colors or sentiment. Vary blender time for a wide range of results. Some possibilities are dried flowers, botanicals (*see page 66*), ferns (plumose fern available at craft stores), party napkins, used gift tissue wrap, gold or silver threads (old tassels work well), glitter (*see page 76*), or something old, something new (a sentimental add-in; only you have to know what it is and why it's there).

O Print text on vellum overlays unless the surface is consistently smooth and uninterrupted by add-ins (*see page 63*).

O Send invitations in designer envelopes. It will *look* like you spent a fortune, but you'll still save a lot of money.

O See Resources for cardstock and designer envelopes from suppliers that cater to brides.

Make Your Own Envelopes

Since envelopes need to be larger than your folded handmade paper, in most cases you won't make the envelope from handmade paper — unless your note card is small (*see page 59*), or you make handmade paper with a larger mold.

But with all the recycled paper out there to choose from, you've got plenty of alternatives. First find an envelope pattern. If your card is a folded sheet of handmade paper made with a standard 5½" × 8" mold, you can use the template on page 202. Enlarge the template on a copier, then trace it onto an 8½" × 11" sheet of paper. Cut out and fold as instructed on the template.

Another easy option is to take an existing envelope apart at the places where it is glued together. Lay the dismantled envelope flat on a sheet of paper and trace around it. With all of the printed sheets in the world, you have a great selection for making envelopes.

Bud Vase

A handmade vase and handmade flowers — what a great way to show off your handmade paper! The project combines paper casting (*see chapter 7*) with pulp painting (*see chapter 5*).

Materials

- Mold for the vase (example uses a tall shot glass)
- Papermaking supplies (*see page 25*)
- Enough pulp to cover your mold
- Vegetable oil for a release agent (spray or apply with a paper towel)
- Handmade paper scraps for flowers
- Flower-shaped paper punch
- Wire for flower stems
- Clear or double-sided tape
- Dried rice or beans

Instructions

1. Determine how much pulp you will need to cover your mold. For example, if your shot glass is 4″ tall and 3″ around, then you will need a pulp shape that is 5″ tall and 3½″ wide (it must be a little larger to allow for overlap).

2. Set up the papermaking screen and support screen over a tray or other container for drainage (*see page 79*). Pour the pulp onto the screen and use pulp layering or painting techniques to create a design. Use a frame for straighter edges, if desired.

3. Apply the release agent to the glass mold, and lay it on its side on top of the pulp. Pull up the screen to roll the pulp around the glass. With the glass upside down, join the pulp on the side and bottom of the glass.

4. With the screen on top of the pulp, use a sponge to blot all the way around the glass. Do not press too hard, as paper may slip on the greasy surface.

5. Once the shape seems quite secure, remove the screen and allow the pulp to air dry, or dry in a 150°F oven for an hour or two. *Note:* Drying in the oven only works if the mold is glass, ceramic, or metal, not plastic!

6. Using scraps from other projects, punch out some paper flowers, tape wire on their backs, and place them in the bud vase. Another option is to use double-sided tape to attach a second flower on the back, to hide the wire. Use dried rice or beans in the bottom of the bud vase to stabilize it and to hold the wire stems in place.

Decision Maker

This could be a fun birthday party game — use the Decision Maker like a fortune teller. Kids can ask the spinner questions and see what it says! The project uses a combination of pulp layering (*see page 78*) and surface embedment (*see page 64*), with a circular mold (*see* Tin Can Papermaking, *page 42*).

Materials

- O Patterned paper scraps for embedded letters
- O Papermaking supplies (*see page 25*)
- O Circular mold, about 6" across
- O Handmade paper scraps for arrow and spacer
- O Straight pin with a decorative tip
- O Pliers
- O Masking or clear tape
- O Scrap of stiff paper or thin cardboard

Variation

This project is easily converted into a toy paper clock. Cut out the numbers 1 through 12, and cut out two arrows (of different lengths) instead of one.

Instructions

1. Cut out the letters for YES, NO, and the question marks. Test them for size to make sure they will fit well onto the circle you will be making.

2. Pour pulp into the circular mold and remove the mold. Do not press out any water yet.

3. One at a time, dip the letters into pulpy water to coat them with fibers, and then press them into the circular sheet.

4. Process and press the paper as usual.

5. When the paper is dry, make an arrow shape and a circular spacer (which will help the arrow spin more freely).

6. Push the pin through one end of the arrow, the center of the spacer, then the center of the large paper circle. Use pliers to bend the end of the pin 90 degrees. Make sure the unbent portion is long enough to allow the parts to move freely. Secure the pin tip with tape, and tape a piece of stiff paper over the pin tip, for safety.

Spinwheels

This classic kid's toy is even more special when made you make it yourself. Just be sure to use handmade paper that is sturdy enough to take some action! The paper can be made with a square mold (an old picture frame with the glass and backing removed), or with standard molds and then cut to size. The instructions are for one pinwheel, but make as many as you like!

Materials

- Handmade paper, 5″ or 6″ square
- Handmade paper scraps
- Flower-shaped hole punch (optional)
- Straight sewing pin with decorative tip
- Colored straw
- Pliers
- Masking or clear tape

Instructions

1. Trim the edges of the handmade paper as needed to make a perfect square.

2. Using the diagram as a guide, draw two diagonal lines to form an X, from corner to corner across the paper. Draw a circle (about ¾″ across) in the exact center, or trace a penny there. Cut from each corner to the edge of the circle; *do not cut* inside the circle.

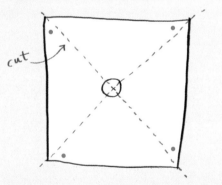

3. From paper scraps, punch a flower shape, or cut out a decorative shape that you like for the center of the pinwheel. Using the straight pin, pierce a hole in the center and set it aside.

4. Use the straight pin again to pierce holes in the exact center of the square, and in every other tip on the square (as marked by small holes on the diagram).

5. Thread the straight pin through the flower shape. Fold the pierced tips of the square into the center, and thread the pin through the holes, from front to back.

6. Push the pin through top of the straw. Use pliers to bend the pin 90 degrees, and secure the pin to the straw with small piece of tape.

Special Seed Card

Seed Cards are a fun way to expand your papermaking experiments. These cards can be sent to your friends and then planted in the ground. With luck and the right conditions, the seeds will sprout and grow! For more about seed papers, including which seeds work best, see Frequently Asked Questions on page 63.

Materials

O Dried flower (the example uses a California poppy)

O Papermaking supplies (*see page 25*)

O String scrap for the stem

O Seeds (the example uses poppy seeds)

Crafty Tip

If you want a folded card to fit in an envelope, be sure to place the flower on one half of the card to leave room for the fold. Use a bone folder to score the card before folding (*see page 148*).

Instructions

1. Prepare the flower by ironing it between two pieces of paper towel. This will remove moisture and make it nice and flat, enabling you to better control how it looks on the card.

2. Make a sheet of paper. While the pulp is still very wet, press the flower into the paper. Lightly dip the string in pulpy water to coat it with fibers, and press it in place as well.

3. Sprinkle the card with seeds.

4. Blot and dry the paper as usual.

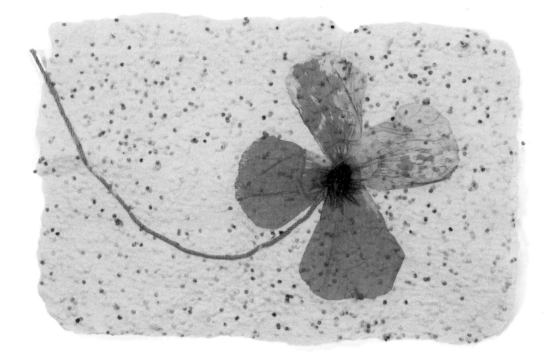

Wacky Bodies

If you like collage, here's a sure-fire way to have a lot of fun with surface embedment (*see page 64*). Grab a stack of magazines and some scissors, and go crazy!

Materials

- Papermaking supplies (*see page 25*)
- Body parts cut from magazines

Instructions

1. Plan your wacky body by laying the pieces out on a table. Make sure the body will fit on the size paper you will be making.

2. Make the pulp for a sheet of paper, but save a bit of the pulp in a small container. Make a sheet of paper, through step 5 (*see page 54*), leaving the sheet very wet for now. Dip each of the cutouts into a thin slurry of the pulp you saved, then drop them one by one onto the surface of the wet sheet. Fibers picked up by the dipping, plus the natural absorption of fibers, will securely tie the cutouts to the sheet.

3. Blot and dry the paper as usual.

4. When the paper is dry, use it as a greeting card or gift artwork.

resources

Arnold Grummer Online

Arnold Grummer's Paper Making
www.arnoldgrummer.com
Arnold Grummer's official website offers paper-making supplies, projects, contests, Ask Arnold, lesson plans for teachers, links, and more.

Arnold Grummer's YouTube Channel
www.youtube.com/arnoldgrummer
Short tutorials with Arnold Grummer include basic papermaking and easy techniques — and he makes it look so easy!

Arnold Grummer's Facebook Page
www.facebook.com/arnoldgrummer
See and share papermaking discoveries, photos, and activities. Post your paper creation!

Buying Information

Check your local art or craft dealer for paper-making supplies. Mail order resources are listed below. Many sites offer papermaking classes and workshops regularly. Check listings in your local community for a hands-on experience near you.

Kits and Supplies for Home and Classroom

Arnold Grummer's Paper Making
800-453-1485
www.arnoldgrummer.com

Dick Blick Art Materials
800-828-4548
www.dickblick.com

Earth Guild
800-327-8448
www.earthguild.com

Nasco Arts & Crafts
800-558-9595
www.enasco.com/artsandcrafts

Paper Alice
937-667-0787
www.paperalice.com

School Specialty, Inc.
888-388-3224
www.schoolspecialty.com

Triarco Arts & Crafts
800-328-3360
www.etriarco.com

United Art and Education, Inc.
800-322-3247
www.unitednow.com

Kits and Supplies for Artists and Studio Papermakers

Carriage House Paper
800-669-8781
www.carriagehousepaper.com

Dieu Donne Papermill
212-226-0573
www.dieudonne.org

Magnolia
510-839-5268
www.magnoliaeditions.com

The Papertrail
800-421-6826
www.papertrail.ca

The Paperwright
613-422-5667
www.paperwright.com

Twinrocker Handmade Paper
800-757-8946
www.twinrocker.com

Other Papermaking Resources

Hand Papermaking Chat Groups

Interesting discussion, valuable archives, resources, and links. Beginners through professional artists welcome.

Friends of Dard Hunter Discussion Group
dardhunter@yahoogroups.com

PaperMaking Forum
papermaking@yahoogroups.com

Organization

Friends of Dard Hunter, Inc.
720-318-6581
www.friendsofdardhunter.org
Dedicated to education and sharing information about the art, craft, history, science and technology of papermaking and related arts. Regional, national, and international meetings include hands-on workshops and presentations.

Special Publication

Hand Papermaking
800-821-6604
www.handpapermaking.org
Advancing traditional and contemporary ideas in the art and craft of making paper.

Interactive Paper Museum

Paper Discovery Center
920-380-7491
www.paperdiscoverycenter.org
Explore the world of paper with a look at its past, its future, and the role paper plays in all facets of our lives. Interactive displays and a hands-on paper lab.

Paper Museums

The Crane Museum of Paper Making
Crane & Co.
Dalton, Massachusetts
413-684-7780
www.crane.com
Exhibits trace the history of American papermaking from Revolutionary times. Crane makes paper for U.S. currency.

Dard Hunter Studios
Chillicothe, Ohio
740-779-3300
www.dardhunter.com
Dard Hunter's Mountain House home and working studio.

Historic RittenhouseTown
Philadelphia, Pennsylvania
215-438-5711
www.rittenhousetown.org
This museum is the site of the first paper mill in America.

Museum of International Paper History
Carriage House
Brookline, Massachusetts
617-232-1636
www.papermakinghistory.org
International collection of books, handmade paper, and artifacts used in the making of paper.

Paper Centers

Robert C. Williams Paper Museum
Institute of Paper Science and Technology
Atlanta, Georgia
www.ipst.gatech.edu/amp
Internationally renowned resource on the history of paper and paper technology with over 10,000 watermarks, books, papers, tools, machines, and manuscripts. Features the Dard Hunter Collection of artifacts and books on paper and hand papermaking.

Beginner classes to advanced studies (even degrees!) in papermaking.

Center for Book & Paper Arts
Columbia College
Chicago, Illinois
312-369-6630
www.colum.edu/Book_and_Paper

Center for the Book
University of Iowa
Iowa City, Iowa
319-335-0447
www.uiowa.edu/~ctrbook

Morgan Art of Papermaking
Cleveland, Ohio
216-361-9255
www.morganconservatory.org

Pyramid Atlantic Art Center
Silver Spring, Maryland
301-608-9101
www.pyramidatlanticartcenter.org

Suggested Reading List

○ **Barrett, Timothy.** *Japanese Papermaking.* Weatherhill, NY, 1983.

○ **Bell, Lilian A.** *Plant Fibers for Papermaking, 8th ed.* Liliaceae Press, McMinnville, OR, 1995.

○ **Flowers, Diane D.** *Handmade Paper from Naturals.* New York: Lark, 2009.

○ **Grummer, Arnold E.** *Paper by Kids, rev ed.* Minneapolis: Dillon Press, 1990.

○ **Heller, Jules.** *Papermaking, 4th ed.* New York: Watson-Guptill, 1985.

○ **Hercher, Gail P.** *Crafting with Handmade Paper.* Gloucester, MA: Rockport Publishing, 2000.

○ **Hiebert, Helen.** *The Papermaker's Companion.* North Adams, MA: Storey Publishing, 2000.

○ ———. *Papermaking with Garden Plants & Common Weeds.* North Adams, MA: Storey Publishing, 2006.

○ **Hunter, Dard.** *Papermaking: The History and Technique of an Ancient Craft, 2nd ed.* New York: Dover, 1978.

○ **Koretsky, Elaine.** *Color for the Hand Papermaker.* Brookline, MA: Carriage House Press, 1983.

○ **Mason, John.** *Papermaking as an Artistic Craft.* London: Faber and Faber, 1959.

○ **Studley, Vance.** *The Art and Craft of Handmade Paper.* New York: Van Nostrand Reinhold, 1977.

○ **Toale, Bernard.** *The Art of Papermaking.* Worcester, MA: Davis Publications, 1983.

○ **Tsien, Tsuen-Hsuin.** *Written on Bamboo and Silk, 2nd ed.* Chicago: University of Chicago Press, 2004.

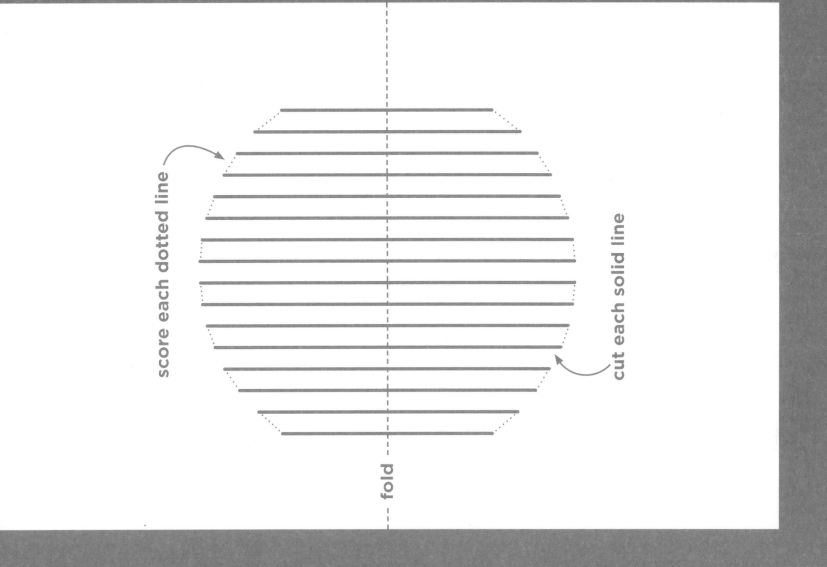

5.5"

score each dotted line

cut each solid line

fold

9.75"

fold

fold

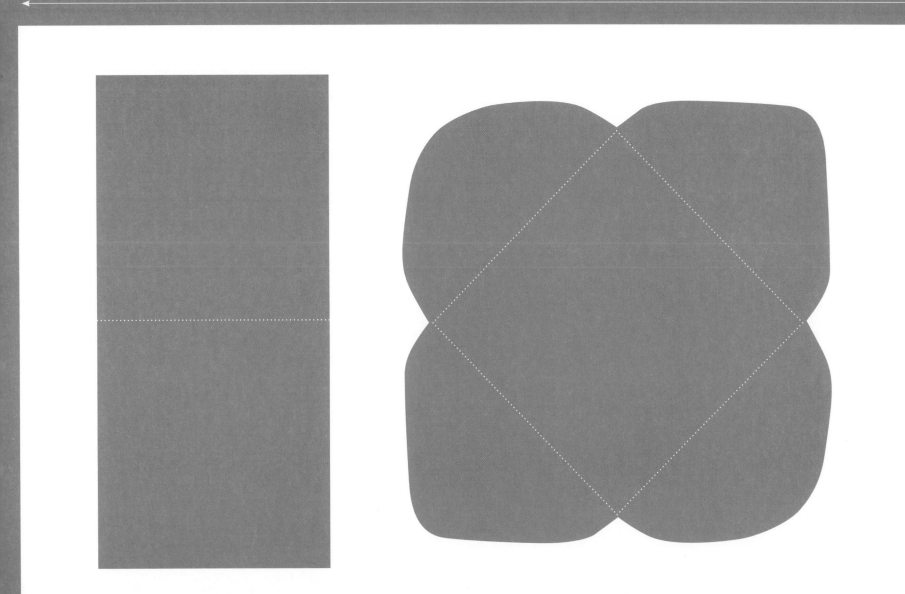

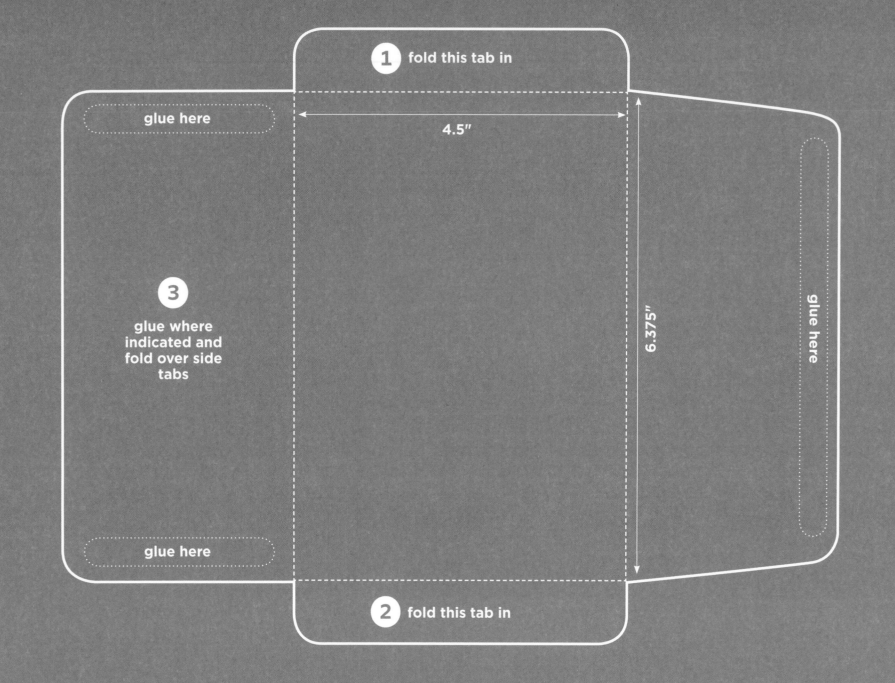

80% scale (enlarge at 125%)

1 fold this tab in

glue here

4.5"

3

glue where
indicated and
fold over side
tabs

6.375"

glue here

glue here

2 fold this tab in

index

acknowledgments

This book would not exist were it not for my daughter, Kim Schiedermayer. She envisioned it, marketed it, and served as liaison with the publisher. Most of all, she spent those necessary endless hours going through over a thousand handmade sheets to select the optimum illustration of a specific technique or point. Then there are drawers and containers full of sculptures, castings, and assorted weirdos. The selection process was pure, unadulterated mental labor of decision after decision after decision. So I repeat, my forever thanks to Kim.

Where can an author do better than at Storey Publishing? I didn't know a publishing staff could be so pleasant, willing, and easy to talk with, and still be so professional and decisive (makes me want to write another book). Our compliments and appreciation to, and my admiration for, Pam Art and Deborah Balmuth, who decided the world needed this papermaking book and performed the labor and judgment to create one. Thanks and admiration also to Nancy Wood, the capable and insightful editor who took on the unimaginable task of combing through my former texts to glean and organize the best from them into the book you now hold. And for giving the book the vital assets of design; my thanks to art director, Dan Williams; the photographer, Greg Nesbit; and stylist, Sara Gillingham.

Acknowledgement must go also to my former colleagues, the entire research staff and faculty of the former Institute of Paper Chemistry. For 17 glorious years they stuffed my brain with cutting-edge paper science and technology for my editorial duties. To delineate the magnitude of their contribution to this book would take another book. The Institute was also the source of the amazing photo on page 10.

I acknowledge the life-long labor of Dard Hunter, master paper historian and founder of the Dard Hunter Paper Museum. It constitutes the world's major collection of paper historical matter (now housed in the Robert C. Williams Paper Museum at the Georgia Institute of Technology). I had the privilege of being its curator for six years. Without that experience, the void in my hand-papermaking knowledge would be endless.

Every would-be author should have benefit of longtime friends in his/her field of expertise, such as I have had. Thanks for Howard and Kathryn Clark of Twinrocker Handmade Paper, the late Joe Wilfer, Dard Hunter III of the Dard Hunter legacy, and each and every member of the vibrant paper craft and art fellowship, Friends of Dard Hunter. They are a fellowship that causes one to keep standards high.

Where would any author be without his spouse? I have Mabel. As long as she can maintain her unbelievably high level of patience and tolerance, we will always be able to look forward to another wedding anniversary. Selah.

Credits: Fish Bowl (page 144), Torrent Lampshade (page 183), and Coiled Bowl (page 185), by Ellie Schiedermayer. Other projects reflect designs by Mary Ayres, Saundra Galloway, Erikia Ghumm, Sara Gillingham, Maria Nerius, and Kay Williams.

Other Storey Titles You Will Enjoy

The Handmade Marketplace, by Kari Chapin.
The must-have marketing guide for motivated artisans!
224 pages. Paper. ISBN 978-1-60342-477-6.

Nature Printing, by Laura Donnelly Bethmann.
An in-depth guide to using objects from nature to create lovely, hand-stamped projects.
96 pages. Paper with flaps. ISBN 978-1-58017-376-6.

Paper Illuminated, by Helen Hiebert.
Innovative designs for using handmade paper to make three-dimensional furnishings.
144 pages. Paper with flaps. ISBN 978-1-58017-330-8.

Papermaker's Companion, by Helen Hiebert.
A complete guide to making your own paper with a variety of easy-to-obtain materials — from harvested plants to junk mail.
224 pages. Paper. ISBN 978-1-58017-200-4.

Papermaking with Garden Plants & Common Weeds, by Helen Hiebert.
Illustrated, step-by-step instructions to make exquisite papers in your home kitchen.
112 pages. Paper with flaps. ISBN 978-1-58017-622-4.

These and other books from Storey Publishing are available wherever quality books are sold or by calling 1-800-441-5700.
Visit us at _www.storey.com_.

about the author

Arnold E. Grummer is the founder and president of Arnold Grummer's Papermaking, a leading supplier of papermaking kits and equipment for home and classroom use since 1976. He has served on the faculty and staff of the Institute of Paper Chemistry and as curator of the Dard Hunter Paper Museum. His educational program clients have included the FBI, the IRS, the American Society for Questioned Document Examiners, the Smithsonian Institution, and the Chicago Museum of Science and Industry. He has made numerous national television and convention appearances, and delivered school programs at every level from Montessori preschool to graduate school. He is the author of four paper-craft books. He lives in Wisconsin with his wife, Mabel.